ORCHIDS
AS HOUSE PLANTS

SECOND REVISED EDITION

REBECCA TYSON NORTHEN

DOVER PUBLICATIONS INC., New York

Published in Canada by General Publishing Com-
pany, Ltd., 30 Lesmill Road, Don Mills, Toronto,
Ontario.
Published in the United Kingdom by Constable and
Company, Ltd.

This Dover edition, first published in 1976, is a new
revised edition of the work originally published by
the D. Van Nostrand Company, Inc., Princeton,
in 1955.

International Standard Book Number: 0-486-23261-1
Library of Congress Catalog Card Number: 75-27673

Manufactured in the United States of America
Dover Publications, Inc., 180 Varick Street
New York, N.Y. 10014

PREFACE

Orchids are blooming in living rooms, sun porches, and basements all across the country. Among the myriad kinds there are some for almost any location, and the nice thing about them is that they do flower. Not only that, but their blossoms often last longer than those of the usual house plants. Their requirements are not hard to meet and their culture is not difficult, although, as for any plants, the grower must learn how to care for them.

It's easier to grow orchids now than it was twenty years ago. This book has been revised to present the methods by which thousands of people are successfully cultivating them in the home. It introduces many of the fascinating kinds that do well as house plants, explains what they need in the way of temperature, light, and humidity, and suggests ways in which their requirements can be met—in windows and orchid cases, and under artificial lights. It tells how to pot, divide, water, and fertilize them and what materials to use. Problems, ailments, and pests that are occasionally troublesome are described, and methods of control are given.

Growing and flowering some of the exquisite species and hybrids offer unparalleled pleasure and excitement. With the basic information contained herein, the amateur can build a new and intriguing plant hobby, and expand it through the years.

I am grateful to Don Wiest for drawings made for the first edition, many of which are used again, and to Abbie Current for new drawings made for this revised edition.

All of the photographs in the book, including the one on the cover, are my own.

REBECCA TYSON NORTHEN

Laramie, Wyoming
March 12, 1975

CONTENTS

ORCHIDS
AS HOUSE PLANTS

CHAPTER I

ORCHIDS AS HOUSE PLANTS

Gardeners want plants in the home as well as outdoors, and even those who own a greenhouse find that plants are still a necessity in the house. Orchid growers are not an exception, and we are typical examples ourselves. We had orchids in the house for more than a year before we had our first greenhouse. Our interest expanded so rapidly that soon we had to have a second greenhouse. Whenever something particularly pretty or interesting would flower we would bring it in the house to enjoy, returning it to the greenhouse when it finished blooming. But that was not enough. We found that even with the greenhouses, we wanted to grow some plants in the house, partly out of curiosity to see what kinds would do well, partly just to have some orchids with us all the time.

We experimented with various kinds, both on a windowsill and in a glass-enclosed ventilated case, all with natural light. Some did well in one situation, some in the other, and some liked neither. While we were working out what would grow in our living room, other orchid lovers were trying their luck, too. The development of fluorescent lights for plants has greatly helped indoor growers. This method was in its infancy twenty years ago. Now fluorescent lights can be used to augment daylight or can be used entirely alone. It used to be thought that a green-

Fig. 1. *Orchids need a bright window in a home, with several hours of sunlight every clear day.*

house was best for plants. It still is for some, of course—very large plants, or those that demand very high light intensities. However, many will do just as well in a window as in a greenhouse, and some will do even better under lights.

Home owners or apartment dwellers have to begin with what they have. A tall, wide, bright window may give enough light as it is, but if not, the light can be augmented with a fluorescent tube or two. Humidity in your home may be high enough for orchids, but if not, a room humidifier can be used to boost it. Actually, plants furnish humidity for each other, so that if you have a large number in the window, among them some thin-leaved kinds, they may create their own damp microclimate. An enclosure of some sort, of glass or polyethylene film, helps to hold moisture, with care to avoid over-damp conditions.

The popular "light carts" can be used. Some furnish only enough light for kinds that require a low intensity. For those that need more light, the cart can be placed in a window to take advantage of available daylight, or additional tubes can be installed. Fluorescent tubes in brackets, placed over plants on benches, can make up for total lack of daylight. Many amateurs have such setups in a basement, where watering is easy to manage, and the size and variety of their collections often rival those of greenhouse owners.

Orchids in the home are a delicious venture. Solving the problems as they arise may take some ingenuity, but success is all the more sweet for that. And orchids offer the greatest variety to be found in any plant family.

Orchids are fascinating because of their tremendous variety of sizes, colors, shapes, and habits, and their variety of fragrances. There are some 30,000 species, and a mere listing of the hybrids fills several large volumes. Best known are the more showy corsage orchids, some of which are suitable for the house. The familiar cattleya tops the list, of course, because of its large size and handsome ruffled lip and because plants may be had in bloom at any time of the year. Its hybrids now offer yellow, bronze, and red-violet, as well as the usual lavender and white. The large cattleyas are now being crossed with smaller kinds to give waxy, perky blossoms in an even wider range of colors. The flowers last for ten days, sometimes for several weeks. Phalaenopsis, the moth orchid, has sprays of large, round, flat pink, white, or yellow flowers that last on the plant from two to five months. Paphiopedilum, called the lady-slipper because of its pouch-shaped lip, is another long-lasting flower, which looks as if it were carved from wax. It comes usually in greens, yellows, and browns, with spots or stripes of red or purple. A fourth popular corsage orchid is the large cymbidium, which requires too bright light for the house, but can be grown outdoors in the summer and brought in to bloom. Its waxy flowers grow on tall, graceful spikes, in shades of yellow, chartreuse, pink, green, brown, and white. Small cymbidium hybrids are now being made which are more amenable to home culture.

The greatest joy is to branch away from the usual kinds, to explore among the myriad forms and discover their never-ending variety. Among them are little fairy-like blossoms, quaintly humorous at times with tails, horns, whiskers, or fringes, or serenely beautiful. Some are large, bold, luridly colored things that often remind one of animal forms. Some come singly on the stem, others in sprays of hundreds of flowers. Many are so fragrant that they perfume a whole room. The plants themselves, which range in size from large to very small, also have intriguing shapes and habits. Some are true miniatures, which may have flowers large for the plant or almost microscopic.

As different as orchid flowers are in shape, size, and color, they are all built on the same basic pattern. The flowers are next above the iris in the evolutionary scale, having come up from lilylike ancestors to become the most highly specialized flowers in the plant kingdom. Like the lily, they are built with three sepals and three petals. The sepals are the outermost flower parts, which serve as the covering of the bud, and which form the background for the rest of the flower. In the cattleya, and in fact in most kinds, the sepals are more slender and more plain in shape than the petals. Of the three petals in the orchid, one has become so modified that we no longer call it a petal. Instead, it is called the lip, or labellum. The specialization of the lip is one of the modifications that place the orchid high in the evolutionary scale. Nature has done fantastic things with the lip. It is often much larger, more ruffled, more showy, more highly colored than the other flower parts. In some kinds it has been carved into many lobes and is often decorated with horns or tails, crests or teeth.

In an orchid flower you do not find separate stamens surrounding a pistil. Instead, you find a single, fleshy, club-shaped structure called the column, which holds both

FIG. 2. *A cattleya flower shows the basic orchid pattern. The three slender parts are the sepals; the two broader ones to the left and right are the petals; and the larger lower part, the lip. Within the lip can be seen the column.*

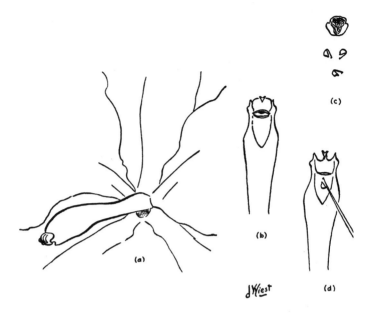

Fig. 3. *The column, typified here by that of a cattleya, contains the anther and stigma, and projects from the center of the flower. The sepals, petals, and lip are attached at its base. Detail of the column: (a) the column (lip of flower removed); (b) the underside of the column showing the anther at its top and below it the stigma; (c) the anther separated from the column and the pollinia removed; (d) the column with one of the pollinia being placed on the stigma to perform pollination.*

the male and female reproductive parts. The column is the hallmark of the orchid, another specialization that gives the orchid its distinction in the evolutionary scale. No matter how strange in appearance a flower may be, or how little it resembles anything with which you are familiar, if you find the reproductive organs fused into a column, you can know you have an orchid. At the tip of the column is a little cap which houses the pollen masses. The pollen grains are held together by wax to form hard pellets, called pollinia. There may be two, four, or eight of them. Below the cap is a shiny depression, and if you touch it with a match stick you will find that it contains a thick, sticky fluid. This is the stigma, the receptive part of the female organ, which receives the pollinia. The "stem" of the orchid flower is actually the ovary, which develops into the seed pod after pollination.

Orchids fall into three general groups as far as temperature requirements are concerned—"cool," "intermediate," and "warm"—and this must always be considered in choosing kinds to grow. The largest numbers come in the "intermediate" group, and the requirements of this and the "warm" group may be easier to fulfill in a home than those of the "cool" group. No orchid likes a hot, stuffy, or steamy atmosphere, not even the members of the "warm" group. All must have fresh air, good light, and nights somewhat cooler than the days. No orchid, if it is to flower, can be grown on the mantel or on a piano or bookshelf away from the light.

The question of the expense of orchid plants usually worries a prospective grower. You have probably read of fabulous prices having been paid for single plants. This is true only of extremely rare ones, or of plants that have some quality of exceptional value to an orchid hybridist. The average cost of orchid plants is about the same as the cost of many potted flowering plants—an Easter lily, for instance. Many charming and desirable species and many inexpensive hybrids can be had for from $5.00 to $20.00. The prices go up from there, but we do not advise paying more for plants until you learn to grow them, and until you know what kinds you particularly desire. When you have learned the habits of mature plants, you can try some seedlings. Seedlings offer an opportunity to acquire fine hybrids without a large initial cost, a subject we shall take up further on.

You would enjoy belonging to an accredited orchid society and subscribing to a good orchid publication. In most large cities there is an orchid society, just as there is a rose or a lily society. It is a lot of fun to meet other orchid growers, to discuss mutual problems and successes, and to find out what other people are doing. They will welcome you whether you have one plant or a thousand. Many of the local societies are affiliated with the American Orchid Society, Inc., which is international in scope, and many in the West are also affiliated with the Orchid Digest Corporation of California. Both of these organizations publish excellent monthly magazines, in which you will find worthwhile articles on many kinds of orchids, culture methods, new research, the activities of amateurs, and help with problems. Your library probably has copies of these publications, but if not, it would be well worth your while to obtain a single copy of *The American Orchid Society Bulletin* and *The Orchid Digest*. They form the best guide as to where to buy plants and equipment, for the leading orchid growers and dealers in supplies advertise in their pages. Their addresses are: The American Orchid Society, Inc., Botanical Museum of Harvard University, Cambridge, Massachusetts 02138; and The Orchid Digest Corporation, 1739 Foothill Blvd., La Canada, California 91011. If any of the growers are near you it would be well to visit them and to buy plants directly. Otherwise, send for their catalogs.

CHAPTER II

ORCHID PLANTS AND THEIR NEEDS

Orchids grow wild all over the world. They can be found in our own woods and valleys, and even up to 10,000 feet elevation in the Rocky Mountains. The largest numbers grow in the tropics and subtropics, and the ones we cultivate in home and greenhouse come from these regions. Yet even in the tropics there is considerable variety of climate. Some orchids grow in the high Andes, where they are constantly cool and are even covered by frost at night. Many grow in the rain forests and cloud forests at altitudes from 3000 to 9000 feet, where the temperatures stay close to 60° or 70° F; others at elevations on down to sea level at progressively warmer temperatures, often exposed to hot sun and drying winds. Some dwell where the air is only moderately humid; some in very moist places such as on cliffs overhanging rushing streams or on rocky coasts where they are washed by salt spray, or in the Pacific Islands where heavy rainfall is the rule. Some are native to regions where dry and wet seasons alternate. The variety of natural conditions leads, of course, to a variety of habits, and you can readily see that orchids cannot be expected to conform to any one set of rules in cultivation.

Orchids are independent green plants, which make their own sugar by photosynthesis and obtain their min-

eral nutrients from decaying humus material. They are
not parasites.

Some kinds grow on the ground, with their fleshy roots
or tubers in the soil, and these are called terrestrials.
There are among them kinds that require a uniform supply of water all year round, and others that need to be dry
through their dormant season.

Most of the orchids we cultivate, however, are epiphytic. Through long ages of evolution they have become
adapted to life above ground, usually in trees, but often
on rocks. The densely matted vegetation of the jungle
floor denied them the good light and air they needed, and
we shall never know what kinds perished before the
epiphytes we now know developed. There are many kinds
of epiphytes, for instance the bromeliads and the Spanish
moss. The name epiphyte was coined to mean plants that
live on other plants, *epi-* meaning "on," and *phyte* meaning "plant." They use the other plants merely as support
and find, in their crotches or in cracks in the bark, pock-
ets of decaying leaves and bugs and material deposited by
the wind. From these deposits and from bird and animal
droppings the plants obtain the minerals they need. Simi-
larly, rock dwellers find nutrients in the crevices and
among mosses and lichens on the surface. Natives in orchid countries bring in armloads of orchid plants from the
forests and toss them onto their thatched roofs, where
they grow and flower, giving their hosts a roof garden of
unmatched beauty.

Survival would be dubious for the epiphytes, cut off
from ground water in their aerial perches, if it were
not for specialization of structure that enables them to
withstand a certain amount of drying. Some live in areas
where they must withstand drying for many months. Others need endure only a few hours of dryness at a time,
between rains or until dew falls at night. The stems and
leaves of such orchids have become storage places for
water. The fat, thickened stems are more or less bulbous
and have earned the name pseudobulb. The leaves are

usually leathery or fleshy, with a compact inner structure and a heavy outer coat of wax that resists drying. The leaf pores are sunken in pits in the wax, which minimizes the air movement at their openings. In these respects they resemble desert plants. They are able to store water when it is available and draw on it between times. There are other patterns among the epiphytes. Some have thin leaves that fall after the season's growth is made, or which may last only into the next season, leaving the pseudobulb to carry the plant through the dry period. Some which have thick leaves do not have pseudobulbs, and these cannot withstand drying quite so well.

The roots of epiphytic orchids are covered by a whitish spongy coat, called velamen, which serves a number of purposes. It protects the inner conductive channel of the root, it soaks up water that falls upon it and absorbs water from damp air, and it has the ability to cling to any surface it touches. It used to be thought that a plant had two sets of roots, one for absorbing and the other to attach it to its perch. The roots are really all alike, and they all wander to a certain extent. Those that happen to grow into the humus material come in contact, of course, with a greater concentration of minerals, which they absorb. Those that wander over the branch fasten themselves so tightly to the bark that they cannot be pried loose. Other roots that do not happen to find anything to cling to simply hang out in the air. They all absorb water and whatever minerals are brought to them by the rain or by water washing over the branch. In cultivation the roots do not all stay in the pot, as do those of terrestrial plants. They wander down into the potting medium, often growing around and around the inside surface of the pot, or out over the sides, where they hang free, or wind themselves around the outside of the pot as if it were a branch, or even travel along the surface of the bench.

There are two general types of growth, illustrated by the accompanying figures. One type makes new growths each year from a rhizome, or ground stem. Each growth

FIG. 4. *A cattleya plant in flower. The blooms come from the current year's growth. This plant has two leads, one with flowers open, and one with buds just emerging from the sheath. Note the stubs of old sheaths and flower stems on older growths.*

FIG. 5. An orchid plant (a laelia) illustrating sympodial growth habit. Starting from the right you can count the growths made in seven successive years, with the youngest at the left. A bud just showing at the base of the youngest growth will become the next new growth. The thickened stems, or pseudobulbs, arise from a creeping ground stem, or rhizome. The roots grow down from the rhizome. The cut stems at the juncture of leaf and pseudobulb are old flower stems.

produces flowers and terminates its growth, usually in one year, although in a few kinds the process takes longer. This type is called sympodial. The basal part of each new growth becomes an extension of the rhizome. New growths come from buds on this basal part and each new growth produces its own set of roots. After a growth has matured and flowered it does not flower again except in a few kinds. The plants that illustrate the sympodial type are a cattleya and a laelia, a close relative of the cattleya (Figures 4 and 5). At the right-hand side of the latter is the oldest growth, and starting with this you can follow the growths made in each of seven successive years, ending with the most recent at the left end. Note the rhizome, or ground stem, and the roots arising from it. At the base of the youngest growth is the bud, just showing, which will develop into the growth for the current season. The thickened oval stems are the pseudobulbs, and in this plant each bears one leaf. From the juncture between the leaf and the pseudobulb the flower stem arises. A sympodial orchid that does not have pseudobulbs is the paphiopedilum, a terrestrial kind.

The other type of growth habit does not have a rhizome and does not make separate new growths each season. Instead, it has a single stem that increases its height throughout its life. This type is called monopodial. New leaves are formed at the growing tip, and flowers arise from the axils of the leaves near the top. Aerial roots are produced from the nodes along the stem. Branch stems may come from the main stem, and these, too, increase in length each year as does the main stem. The plant used to illustrate the monopodial type is a vanda (Figure 6). It grows tall rapidly by lengthening its stem and adding many leaves each year. Eventually it grows too tall to be handled conveniently, and loses many of its lower leaves, at which time the top part can be cut off and repotted to start the plant anew. As new roots form they give the plant a new foothold. Another monopodial you will meet is phalaenopsis, which adds only a leaf or two a year and does not grow as tall as vanda.

We cannot help changing the environment of orchids when we move them from their native haunts into our homes. Just growing them in pots is a drastic change, as is moving them into a region of short winter days and long summer days. Substituting artificial heat for the soft damp air of the tropics is still another change. Let us, for just one example, compare the native habitat of the cattleya with conditions under which we must grow it. It comes from the South American rain forests, from an altitude of from 3000 to 6000 feet. There the days are close to twelve hours long all year round, and the temperature varies only a few degrees from 70°F, day and night, win-

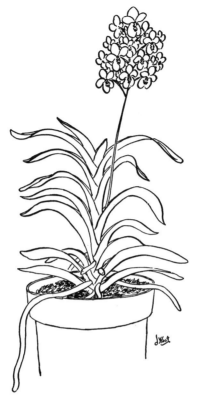

Fig. 6. *An orchid plant (a vanda) illustrating monopodial growth habit. It has one main stem that grows taller and adds more leaves at its tip year after year. Side branches may come from the main stem, and these continue growth in the same manner. Flower stems are produced from leaf axils along the stem, as are aerial roots.*

ter and summer. It lives in the branches of tall trees, receiving bright light all day with some shade from moving leaves at noon, and free circulation of clean air. The roots penetrate a thin layer of mosses and lichens or wander over the exposed branch, and thus have perfect drainage. There is always dew at night and almost always a daily shower. Between times, the sun dries off the plants and their roots.

These conditions are difficult to imitate; in fact, we

cannot entirely do so. It has been found that the plants do poorly when we give them a temperature of close to 70°F at night. Our summer days run to 90°F and above, and we cannot help it. Fortunately, the cooler mornings and evenings keep the plants from becoming depleted. Our winters offer short days, fewer hours of light than the tropics give, with spells of dark weather in many regions. If we water the plants in pots as frequently as they receive water in their native perches, the potting medium becomes soggy and the roots waterlogged.

It has been necessary to work out a new set of conditions to suit each kind of orchid, conditions that differ somewhat from their native environment, but which still furnish them what they need. For instance, although cattleyas have a night temperature of perhaps 68° in the rain forests, we find that they do better for us with a night temperature of between 55° and 60° in the winter, with somewhat warmer summer nights. We may give only a weekly watering instead of the daily shower. And so on.

One problem for the early growers was to find something to use as a potting medium that would give the plants the extremely free root aeration they need, yet also furnish them with minerals. Soil is too compact for the epiphytes. Even the terrestrials, which natively grow in the ground, need a more porous medium than our other house plants because they come from the light, fluffy medium of leaf mold and rotten wood offered by the forest floor. After many trials and errors, it was found that osmunda fiber, the roots of the osmunda fern, was an excellent medium. Its fibers are tough so that no matter how tightly the medium is compressed it still allows good air circulation. It is a dead plant material, and as it slowly decays it gives the plants the necessary minerals. Its fibers hold water, and if watered carefully furnish the roots contact with a damp medium. Osmunda fiber, however, is tedious to use, and moreover has become scarce and very expensive. It is still used for plants in baskets and for an occasional one that does not tolerate other media. A search for less costly, easier-to-use materials turned up chopped bark, tree-fern fiber, even gravel and volcanic rock. The latter two are frequently used where orchids are grown outdoors in places with heavy rainfall, the former in greenhouses and homes.

Although most orchids have a fairly wide range of tolerance to day temperatures, night temperatures are critical. We shall emphasize the night temperatures for each kind we discuss. Your success with whatever kinds you decide to try will be better insured if you are careful about the night temperatures. A kind that will grow and flower with a night temperature of 55° to 60°F may not flower if kept at 65° at night. Another that will flower when grown with a night temperature of 50° will not flower when the nights are allowed to run above that. The "intermediate" and "warm" orchids comprise a tremendous variety of kinds, whose night temperature requirements of 55° to 60° and 60° to 65° can usually be met in the home better than those of the "cool" group. But even in this range 5° makes a difference—often between flowers and no flowers, thrifty growth and poor growth.

Light is necessary to make sugar. Sugar is not only the energy food of plants, but the start in the long line of chemicals manufactured by the plant. Fractions of the sugar molecule are combined with minerals from the growing medium to make proteins, pigments, hormones, enzymes, perfumes, etc. A plant that does not have enough light to enable it to make a supply of sugar to meet all these demands cannot grow and flower satisfactorily. It may make only vegetative growth, or if it flowers, the flowers may be of poor quality. We are content with ivy and philodendron, schefflera and sansevieria for their foliage alone. But if we know that a plant can flower in the home we are not happy unless it does so. Furnishing orchids with good light is one of the most vital factors in growing them successfully; they make more thrifty, sturdy growth, better root systems, and more flowers of better color and substance.

Humidity is a problem each grower more or less has to work out for himself, and we shall make suggestions for the individual kinds. We have found that plants in the home seem to need a somewhat lesser relative humidity than in a greenhouse. This may be due to the fact that they receive less strong light in the home, or that there is not such a wide range between day and night temperatures, or possibly that the air in the house is more still than it is in a greenhouse. Whatever the answer, we feel that many indoor growers worry too much about humidity for their plants, and often overdo it. Unhealthy conditions can arise from keeping the plants in a nearly saturated atmosphere. A glass case, or a polyethylene partial case, protects the plants from drying air currents and allows a higher humidity to build up. Some kinds do not need this extra protection, and an occasional mist spray over the foliage usually will make up for the low humidity of the house. Whenever orchids are grown in an enclosed volume of air, careful ventilation is necessary. It is better in general to let the humidity rise and fall at intervals than to keep it at a constant level.

Most orchids make new growth during the spring and summer, when the days are increasing in length. Some get a head start by beginning in January, whereas others do not start new growth until May or June, but almost all orchids are showing swelling "eyes" or well-started young growths by March. New root activity accompanies the new growth. Some kinds flower almost as soon as new growth begins, even before the leaves have reached full length, others wait to produce flower stems until fall or winter, and still others until the following spring. There are deciduous kinds that mature the pseudobulb and flower as the leaves begin to fall or after they have fallen. Hybrids may inherit the habit of one or another of their ancestors.

Most orchids have some period during their year's cycle when they appear to be inactive. We do not like to think of this as actual inactivity, but rather as lessened activity. It is sometimes called a rest period. It is a time when the plant is not visibly accomplishing anything; when it is neither making vegetative growth nor producing flowers. However, changes are going on in the plant in preparation for activity to come, and these changes, though too subtle for us to see, are important. During the period of lessened activity plants that retain their leaves are still making sugar, roots are absorbing water and minerals, and internal cells are manufacturing the various chemicals necessary to the working of the plants. While they may need less water, they still require some, so we put them on a schedule of less frequent watering. Plants that lose their leaves go into a more definite dormant period, some even requiring no water at all from leaf fall until start of new growth. Individual needs for seasonal changes will be taken up later.

In Chapter III we shall use cattleyas as the basic examples of habit and culture, and for other kinds (Chapters VI and VII) we shall note where necessary how they differ from cattleyas in handling. But first we must discuss the installation and lighting problems relevant to all orchids.

WINDOWS
AND CASES

When we first obtained an orchid case we put some mature and nearly mature cattleyas in it, thinking that they would do better than a group which had already spent a successful year on a windowsill. To our surprise, those in the case did not do as well as those that were unprotected. The growths were softer and more slender, and came blind, that is, failed to flower. Studies with a light meter showed that plants in the case received considerably less light than those on the windowsill, partly because they were farther back from the window and partly because the light had to come through two thicknesses of glass. The plants in the case had had a higher relative humidity than those in the window, but without enough light to make a good supply of food (sugar), they were unable to make as strong growth or produce flowers. It would seem from this (and we have seen many other such examples) that, if a case is to be used, it must be given exceptionally good light, or the light must be augmented in some way. Otherwise, cattleyas and other light-demanding kinds will do better directly in a window, perhaps with supplemental light, or under entirely artificial light.

Nearly mature seedlings have the same requirements as adult plants and can be included with them in the following directions. There is no difference in culture between species and hybrids.

WINDOWS

LIGHT. Light for growing orchids is usually given in footcandles. Some photographic light meters have a conversion table, often used with an attachment, by which footcandles can be measured. General Electric makes one that reads in footcandles directly. Plants that are light-demanding need 2500 to 3000 footcandles; those that thrive with a moderate intensity do well with 1500 to 2000 footcandles; and those that need even less, will accept around 1000. For convenience we shall call these three ranges high, medium, and low light. Many kinds of orchids are happy with intensities somewhere in between. A chart for use with artificial light is given in Chapter IV. A grower should know approximately how much light his setup offers and choose kinds that are suitable, or, if he has an affinity for some particular orchids, he should prepare to meet their needs.

In practice, the plants themselves will tell whether they are receiving enough or too little light. With too little, the growths may be weak and floppy; leaf color may be either very dark green, or, if the light is really dim, a pale yellow. With plenty of light, the growths will be sturdy, the color a lively green, and the leaves upright. It is interesting to watch a plant that is weak from insufficient light straighten up and become strong when given better light.

The larger the window, the more plants can be grown in it and the better light they will have. If the window is narrow, and therefore unable to give as many hours of good light, plants that are not demanding of truly bright light should be chosen. A room that is all windows, such as a sun room or solarium, is ideal, of course. In a particularly bright exposure you may even be able to grow light-demanding kinds such as cymbidiums, and certainly cattleyas and many others that need excellent light.

Prepare the setting by installing something to catch drip from the pots—either a metal tray the same size as the sill, or a frame with a covering of plastic. If the former is possible, it would be a great advantage to have a drainage tap built in. Perhaps the sill is not broad enough to be thus used, in which case a planter-table can be placed in front of the window, or stands to hold the pots. Isolated plants are harder to take care of than plants in groups, however. The metal tray or planter-table can be deep enough to hold water in the bottom to help with humidity; a rack made of redwood slats or hardware cloth placed over the water keeps the plants from standing in it, yet lets moist air surround the pots.

Plants in a house usually do not have the long hours of light possible in a greenhouse. Therefore, the aim is to give them at least several hours of direct sun every clear day. Even better than a single large window is a double exposure, especially one afforded by corner windows facing east and south, allowing good light winter and summer, and longer hours. The danger of direct sun is that if it is too hot it can burn or bleach the leaves. The leaves absorb light and become warmer than their surroundings, and they may become scorched. A leaf burn is at first a dry, brownish patch that later turns dark brown and then black. Too much light continually, even without extreme heat, causes the leaves to become yellow and dry-looking, sometimes with a bronzy tinge. Such yellowing must be distinguished from that due to overwatering. Feel the leaves when the sun is shining on them, and if they feel hot draw a piece of cheesecloth (double thick) or some other type of thin mesh curtain across the window to break the light. The plants will thus receive direct sun in a broken pattern. Watch out for heat in a bay window particularly.

Cattleyas, and any other light-demanding kinds you may choose, must have the most advantageous positions in the window; they must receive sun as early and as late as possible. Less light-demanding kinds may receive enough for their needs when they are set between and somewhat farther back than the former. Light intensity falls off with increasing distance from the glass, so be careful not to keep plants too far from the window. Various means can be used to bring plants closer to the light —hanging them from the frame (top or side), raising them on stands so that they are not in the shadow of others, or placing shelves across the window for them. Plants that have pendent flower sprays have to be raised up anyhow.

What to do if you discover that the plants are suddenly too hot? Give them a quick mist of water, which in itself helps cool them, and promotes further cooling as it evaporates from the leaves. Move them out of the heat or increase the shade. Ventilation and air circulation are important aids, about which more below.

TEMPERATURE. In speaking of temperature (and of any other environmental condition) we have to realize that the ideal cannot always be attained. Yet it is of value to know what the ideal is, in order to come as close to it as possible. Cattleyas do their best when they can have a night temperature of between 55° and 62°F through the winter, and this is ideal for others of the "intermediate" range. These moderately cool night temperatures allow the best growth to be made. Higher night temperatures tend to deplete the food reserves of the plant, using food that should be saved for flower formation. In a greenhouse, the night temperatures can be controlled for the benefit of the plants, but homes are built and managed for the comfort of their human occupants. In a greenhouse, the temperature drops as the sun goes down. In a home the furnace is not turned down until the occupants go to bed. Also, in a home the temperature does not fall as rapidly as in a greenhouse, and the plants do not have as many cool hours as they do in a greenhouse. However, conditions in general are less rigorous in a home than in a greenhouse—for instance, there are not the extremes of temperature, nor the need for as free ventilation in the summer to offset the long hours of sun heat. With the more equable environment of a home, the plants seem to be able to tolerate night temperature a bit above what is considered ideal. This does not mean that night temperature should be ignored, for cattleyas will grow and flower more successfully the closer you can come to the ideal conditions. But it does' mean that if you cannot furnish a place for them where the temperature drops to 55° to 62°F at night, come as close as you can, and try to keep the temperature under 65°F at night. If you cannot meet these requirements, you would do better to try the delightful kinds available for warmer temperatures (or cooler if the opposite is true).

Summer day temperatures are tolerated pretty well, with the cooler mornings and evenings to make up for the hotter hours. In addition to burning, mentioned above, another danger of high temperatures is increased evaporation of water from the leaves. Orchids cannot make up extreme water loss as rapidly as garden plants, because absorption by the roots is not fast enough. The leaves do not wilt when dry, but over a long period the leaves and pseudobulbs become thin and somewhat shriveled. It does not pay to pour more water into the pot if the medium is already damp, although the plants will need more frequent watering in hot weather. A light syringing with a mist sprayer when the leaves are warm from the sun will help to make up for loss of water through evaporation. Not only will the plants absorb some of this water, but evaporation from their surfaces will help to cool them. The plants can be syringed in this way several times a day in hot weather, as long as you are careful not to wet the medium too much and contribute to overwatering of the pot.

WATER. It is difficult to give an absolute schedule for watering. As long as the medium is damp the roots can absorb water, either from the moist air between particles or from contact with them. The medium dries out more quickly in warm weather than in cool, and in a dry atmosphere than in a humid one, and in small pots than large ones. As the medium approaches dryness the pot becomes lighter in weight. Try to judge when the medium is *almost* dry, and water then, a system used for cattleyas and kinds with similar needs. We will note later kinds to be kept more damp.

Soak the pot thoroughly when you water; with the plant in the sink, let water from the faucet run over the entire surface several times. Then let the plant drain before putting it back in place. If you have a tray under the plants and a means for removing excess water from it (a drain tube, or a siphon which you can use when needed), you can water the plants in place, again being sure to wet the medium thoroughly each time.

Watering too frequently leads to ill health. A waterlogged medium cannot hold enough air to supply the needs of the roots. When air spaces between the root cells become filled with water, the roots die for lack of oxygen. Leaves become sickly yellow or yellow-green, and watery-looking. Plants may fail to flower or may produce flowers of thin substance that soon fade. Growths become smaller because the roots are unable to absorb enough minerals. Finally, the roots die and rot. When the roots are rotten, the plant wobbles in the pot, and this is often your first clue to damage. When you notice this condition, remove the plant from the pot and cut off the rotten roots, put it in fresh medium, and keep it dry for two or three weeks. Watch the medium, however, so as to avoid such an extreme, and water less frequently if you find that you have been watering before it approached dryness.

FERTILIZER. Various media in which orchids can be grown will be described later. These include chopped bark, tree-fern fiber, etc. Fertilizer must be given with all, preferably one with an N-P-K ratio of 30-10-10, or close to it. Fertilizers (completely water-soluble) especially compounded for orchids are available from orchid dealers. Follow directions, and give at every other watering. Salts can accumulate in the pots and are injurious to roots. Giving plain water in between fertilizing helps keep salts from building up. Also, it is best to water first just before applying the fertilizer to give a second leaching. Fertilizer need not be given to dormant plants. And it should be given less frequently during a prolonged spell of dark weather. Of course, you cannot tell how long dark weather will last, but let us say the days have been dull for two weeks since the last application of fertilizer—skip the fertilizer for that time. If the weather brightens, give it the following week.

HUMIDITY. Humidity is not a problem in a damp climate except when furnace heat dries the air. During winter, or any time in a dry climate, there are means of providing additional humidity. An ideal level to aim for is between 40% and 60%, but the latter may be possible only for short intervals. One method you may have seen described is to stand the pot on a tray of wet gravel. If you wish to try this, we suggest that the "gravel" should be a porous type of rock such as pumice or scoria, so that it will continually draw up water to be evaporated. The water level must be checked carefully so that the pot does not sit in water. It is a good idea to place a rack over the gravel on which to stand the pot. It must be said, however, that this is not a very good way to provide humidity for one lone plant; the amount of moisture that enters the air is slight, and is quickly dissipated. It is better to have a group of plants on a large tray. Algae may grow in the water, and can be controlled by adding a little Physan (the new name for Consan-20) to the water in the tray, following instructions on the bottle as to dilution.

Enclosing the area with plastic curtains helps to hold humidity. Be careful that the curtains do not cut off warmth from the room in cold weather, or hold heat in the summer. A room humidifier or vaporizer can be placed in either the enclosed or unenclosed window, and turned on several times a day. If you are not at home, a time clock can do the job. This raises the humidity intermittently and helps to keep the plants from becoming dehydrated. If the window is full of plants, as we mentioned earlier, there is naturally a higher humidity surrounding them.

In these days of air conditioning, it is difficult to know what to say about open windows. Certainly during mild weather and at night, the plants will benefit from the damp fresh air from outdoors.

ORCHID CASES

There are few commercially made cases on the market, and most growers build their own. The design and materials can vary, but any case to be used for large plants must be tall and hold a large volume of air. A low, small case is good for seedlings or the smaller botanical orchids. Mature cattleya plants, however, especially some of the laeliocattleyas, can be over two feet tall from the bottom of the pot to the tip of the leaves. Many produce tall flowering stems which add even more height. A case in which the tops of the plants touch the glass top would allow no room for flowers. A good size is 2 feet deep, 3 feet long, and 3 feet or more tall. Extra head room not only allows space for taller plants, but has a very real importance in keeping plants healthy. Orchids do not thrive in saturated air. The larger volume of air enclosed by a larger case does not become saturated as easily as that in a small case and does not invite the growth of molds. In a small, close case the plants and pots can become sticky with mold.

Second, the case must have adequate ventilation. Some cases have doors that open at each end, either the hinged or sliding-panel type. Some have the top hinged to swing upward and a door opening at the back or side. We prefer top and bottom ventilation, which allows the heated air to move up and out. The case we use has perhaps the best

Fig. 7. *An orchid case in a living-room window. Note the top and bottom ventilators, as well as the end door. The plant in the extreme left corner is a pleurothallis; next is a young dendrobium, then several phalaenopsis, an oncidium, and a number of miniature orchids on hanging arrangements. A piece of cheesecloth is pulled across the window when the sun is hot. A small room humidifier in the case itself can be turned on once or twice each day when necessary to raise the humidity.*

FIG. 8. *Plastic film over a tubular plastic framework makes this indoor "greenhouse" a possibility for growing orchids. Called "Casabella," it is made by Casaplanta and drawn from their catalog. For orchids it would need more ventilation than offered by the door; an opening in the top might suffice. As with the orchid case in Fig. 7, a thin shade curtain should be used to prevent overheating.*

arrangement of all. A panel at the top is hinged to open upward, and at the bottom on both ends there is a hinged panel that can be opened. This allows a gentle upward movement of air through the case without having to leave either of the end doors open. The end doors give good access to the case for watering and moving plants. If you build your own case, we suggest that you plan to have the ends or the back hinged for this purpose. It is very difficult to reach down through a top opening without breaking flowers or tipping over plants.

At the bottom of the case there should be a pan for catching and holding water. We prefer an open pan, without gravel, as it is easier to clean. Moisture in the pan adds somewhat to the humidity in the case.

A means of giving good light and still having the benefit of a case has been worked out by some amateurs. A partial case is built, by means of a framework fastened around the window. The back, sides, and top are closed by glass or plastic, leaving the front open to the window. Ventilation is provided by hinged doors, or, if a pliable material is used, by rolling back the top and some other section.

A cross between a case and a greenhouse is an extended window, built out from a regular window. It opens into the room on the inside and is worked from the room, although it may be closed at will. Like a greenhouse, it can become extremely hot from sun heat and must have regular greenhouse white shading applied to the glass according to the season. Shading can also be provided by tacking cheesecloth inside to the framework. Even with shading to reduce the heat from the sun the plants will receive more hours of strong light than they can indoors. Ventilation to the outside (a top panel that opens upward and perhaps a side panel that also opens) is a necessity, for there will not be enough circulation back into the room to carry out the heated air. Such a window, exposed on all sides to the elements, may need extra heat in

FIG. 9. *An extended window offers extra light. The glass should probably be painted with white shading compound, as for a greenhouse, unless shaded by trees during the summer. A small humidifier and a fan for air circulation should probably be installed. A lining of polyethylene film would help insulate it in winter. The owner would have to experiment to see whether keeping it open to the dwelling would maintain its temperature at a desirable level winter and summer.*

the winter, which may be obtained by the use of a heating cable and thermostat.

LIGHT. An orchid case, like a greenhouse, has its own little environments even within its small volume. Plants that stand closest to the window will shade those behind them. A plant that stands up tall, or one that hangs, will have better light and a somewhat more dry atmosphere than a low plant or one that stands in a corner. Plants that have different light requirements can be grown together in the same case (providing they all have the same temperature requirement). Those that need the most light can be placed nearer to the window, or raised on overturned pots to allow them to stand up higher. Plants that need less light can be placed toward the back. They will receive less light simply for being farther from the window, so they should not be hidden behind other plants. A few small plants on pieces of cork bark or tree fern can be hung from screws inserted into the framework. They are thus raised higher than plants that stand on the bottom, and their flowers can better be seen. A miniature "tree" made of driftwood might stand in one corner, bearing in its crotches tiny plants bedded on moss or osmunda fiber. These must be watered more often than plants in pots.

The sun shining into a closed case makes it extremely hot in a short time. It is the heat of the sun that is dangerous. When the case becomes hot it must be ventilated at once, or, rather, it should be ventilated before becoming hot. You soon learn to know the seasons—at which times of year the case heats up, and at what time of day to anticipate it. Then, during the hours of heat, open the top and bottom ventilators, and give the plants a mist spray. Watch to see how the temperature runs, and if it is still above 85°F draw a piece of cheesecloth or other mesh material across the window, to cut out some of the light. Try to remove the shade as soon as the sun slants away from the window to allow the plants good light the rest of the day.

Fig. 10. *An orchid "tree" made from a piece of driftwood. Miniature plants are fastened to pads of osmunda fiber or sphagnum moss.*

TEMPERATURE. The temperature requirements are the same as for plants grown on a windowsill. A case can be equipped with a heating element controlled by a thermostat. This makes it possible to keep an orchid case in a location that cools off considerably at night, such as a bedroom or a glassed-in porch, and may enable you to keep the night temperature down closer to the ideal than is possible in a living room. A thermostat must be checked with a thermometer, for it may not be in perfect adjustment with the actual temperature. Either reset the thermostat, or make a calibration so that you know how to regulate it to keep an even temperature.

One word of caution. If the heating element is in the form of a coil or strip at one side or end of the case, be sure that the plants next to it do not become too hot. During the season when the heat must be used, it may be necessary to move the plants back from the element, or raise them up or shield them in some way from the heat.

VENTILATION AND HUMIDITY. These are important phases of running an orchid case. While the case is used primarily to furnish a higher relative humidity than contained in the atmosphere of the home, the plants and the interior of the case must be allowed to dry off at least once a day. Even when temperature conditions do not require opening the ventilators, as described above, they must be opened to allow the air to change. If the ventilators are kept closed for two or three days in a row the pots and plants surfaces become sticky. Algae and fungi develop on the damp surfaces. It is easier to prevent this than it is to get rid of it. A suggestion is to keep a ventilator cracked open during the day and to close the case at night. During the day when the case warms up, it is of course necessary to open the ventilators wider.

It is difficult to name an ideal percentage of relative humidity. Our Wyoming climate is very dry. Ten to fifteen percent relative humidity is about normal, with a rise to 40% when it rains and an occasional drop to 5%. The relative humidity in the closed orchid case usually stands at about 40% from evaporation of water in the pan and from the plants themselves. Just after watering or misting the plants, the humidity will rise to 60% or 70% and will remain so for some time if the case is kept closed. However, while it is good for the plants to have the higher humidity at intervals, we do not like to keep it at this high level for long periods, for in order to do so we must either keep the ventilators closed all the time or wet the plants very frequently. It is better to let the plants be alternately wet and dry; to let the air in the case move out and be replaced with fresher, drier air each day; to mist the plants while the sun is shining on them, with the ventilators open; and then, in the evening, to close the case.

In our dry climate the case dries out more quickly when the furnace is on. We found that a neat solution to the problem was to keep a small vaporizer inside the case and plug it in twice a day for ten or fifteen minutes. This wets the leaves, pots, surface of the medium, and the

glass. In any less dry climate there might be a danger of
mold, but this does not occur for us, possibly because the
case always has air moving through it—from bottom ventilators up and out of a cracked-open top one.

WATERING. Pots in a protected case will not dry out as
fast as those on a windowsill. If by chance any should
become overwatered, as evidenced by rotting roots or yellowing leaves, remove them from the case and let them
dry out thoroughly, repotting if necessary. A plant can
remain out of the case for a couple of weeks without
harm.

PLANTS IN FLOWER. Ventilation is very important
when plants are in flower. It does not hurt the flowers to
have an occasional mist spray of water and, in fact, may
help maintain their freshness. But they must not remain
wet for long. In a close, dank atmosphere a fungus
(*Botrytis*) may develop on the flowers, causing brown or
pinkish spots. Free ventilation will help prevent this. If
some flowers should develop spots, they should be cut off
and destroyed at once to prevent spread of the fungus.
Plants in flower should be watered the same as otherwise,
with the usual care not to overwater.

ENCLOSURES FOR SMALL PLANTS

Small orchids, dwarf or miniature, can have their own
small enclosures, although, of course, they can be grown
along with larger ones in any of the situations just mentioned. Young seedlings would do especially well in small
cases, but older ones can dwell with mature plants. There
is almost no end of ways such enclosures can be made.
They will need ventilation—the smaller they are the more
quickly will the air become saturated. The little case can
stand in a window or have its own artificial lighting, to be
described below.

A simple enclosure can be made by covering a wire or

slat frame with polyethylene film and standing this over a tray holding wet porous rock. One side of the film should be left free as a hanging curtain, to be folded back when too much moisture condenses on the inside. As mentioned earlier, the plants should not stand directly on the wet gravel, but on a rack just above it. Sheets of glass or Plexiglas can be glued together to make a four-sided enclosure to stand over a tray. A lid of the same material but somewhat narrower than the enclosure can be placed on top, with space at the edges for ventilation. If the lid is of the same size, provision should be made for propping it open when necessary. A fish tank can be used in the same way. Excess water can be removed from the tray or the tank by means of a siphon or suction bulb.

Little has been done with terrariums for orchids, and you are on your own if you wish to experiment. We have not tried them ourselves, but can see certain problems that would have to be worked out. Terrariums as used for other kinds of plants are little enclosed worlds which, once planted, maintain their own atmosphere. Orchids, however, even kinds that like to be kept quite damp, need air movement. A container for them should therefore have a large enough opening to allow ventilation, and should not be kept closed all the time. A fish tank makes perhaps the best terrarium because of its open top. The system of planting things directly in the bottom of the terrarium offers the danger to orchids of keeping the roots too wet. You might try it, but be very sure that the medium is only just damp, not sopping, and that no water stands in the bottom. There should be a very deep layer of gravel under the bark. Fertilizer will have to be given at times, which could cause the water level to rise up into the bark. You would have to flood the substrate once in a while to leach out accumulated salts, and then draw off the water.

It would probably be better not to plant the orchids directly in the bottom, but to keep them in their pots well above the substrate. If any did not take to terrarium life they could easily be removed without disturbing the others. They can be attractively arranged by standing them on decorative rocks, or other objects such as small logs, of different heights. If you wish, the terrarium could be additionally "landscaped" with things that can be planted in the substrate, such as small ferns.

With the little enclosures, as with large ones, watch out for overheating when the sun shines on them.

SUMMERING OUT

Growers in warm climates sometimes put their orchids outdoors for the summer, whether they grow them in windows or under lights. Plants that have lived under lights, particularly in basements, may benefit from the few months of natural sunlight, and both these and windowsill ones receive a boost from the freer air movement and gentle, usually damper, night atmosphere. They can be hung from the lower branches of trees so that they receive shade, but there is danger of insects invading them from the trees themselves. It is better to place them on stands or benches under artificial shade, such as saran cloth, or in a corner of a patio where they may receive light in the morning and shade the rest of the day. Protection from the usual garden pests is necessary. Watering has to be handled according to the climate—very little may be needed where rains are frequent, and plants may even have to be protected from too much at times. Be sure they have adequate drainage wherever they are placed. Fertilizing has to be more frequent when the plants are subjected to frequent rains.

CHAPTER IV

GROWING WITH ARTIFICIAL LIGHT

With artificial light you can almost outsmart the sun; certainly you can outsmart the weather. Although lights indoors furnish something less than good sun, they also make up for cloudy days and those dull weeks of winter and spring that prevail in some parts of our country. With electric lights you can grow an astonishing array of orchids. Much has been learned about fluorescent lights, although we still need to know more. We cannot give the final word on their use. In fact, amateurs would not accept word that claimed to be final—experimenting is too much fun. It is helpful, though, to know what is being done as a point from which to start. It has been estimated that in some regions over half the growers cultivate their orchids indoors, and that over half of these use artificial lighting, either entirely or to supplement daylight. Some greenhouse growers use it to brighten a too-shady bench.

Most growers use a combination of fluorescent and incandescent bulbs. The incandescents furnish wave lengths in the red spectrum, necessary for flowering, and missing in many types of fluorescents. The best combination has been cool-white fluorescent and incandescent (plain, not red-coated) in a ratio of at least 1:4, approximately 25 watts of incandescent to 100 watts of fluorescent. Fixtures thus equipped are on the market. A small amount of sun, for example where a plant cart can stand next to a window, can take the place of incandescents.

Fluorescent lamps are being improved now, however, to give more nearly the spectrum needed by orchids, and these are said to be sufficient without the addition of incandescents. New types appear in rapid succession, and those available now will undoubtedly be replaced by better ones as the years go by. Some on the market at the time of this writing carry trade names such as Agro-Lite and Plant-Gro (Westinghouse); Plant Light (General Electric); TruBloom (Verilux); Vita-Lite and Naturescent (Duro-Lite); and Gro-Lux Wide Spectrum (Sylvania). These are produced in various lengths and wattages. We suggest that if plants do not flower well after a reasonable length of time with any of these tubes, you might add the incandescent bulbs in the ratio just mentioned.

Most manufacturers also make fluorescent tubes that give a higher light intensity, called High Output and Very High Output. From the General Electric lamp catalog the following figures have been obtained (those in the Westinghouse and Sylvania catalogs are comparable): High Output (HO) lamps come in many lengths and wattages, all of them 800 milliampere and requiring a fixture made for that amperage; among them are 18-inch 25-watt, 24-inch 35-watt, 36-inch 45 watt, 48-inch 60-watt, 72-inch 85 watt, 84-inch 100-watt, and 96-inch 110-watt. Very High Output (VHO) lamps are 1500 milliampere, and come in 48-inch 110-watt, 72-inch 165-watt, and 96-inch 215 watt, and require a fixture suitable for that amperage. Of the various "color" types offered, the choice would be the cool-white, and these should be combined with the proper ratio of incandescents. The high intensity of this group of lamps allows them to be placed a greater distance above the plants, giving space for taller kinds and flower stems, and also greater ease in working with them.

All tubes must be replaced when their efficiency declines, and this may be at something like one-third of the estimated actual life of the lamp. Plants react to lowered intensity and color change before the human eye would find the intensity unsatisfactory. It is probably best to replace them on a rotational basis.

Fluorescent tubes produce some heat, but far less than incandescent. Leaves may or may not be burned by touching the former, although they should not be in continual contact with them, but they can be badly burned by the latter. The ballasts become especially hot. Ballasts in the small fixtures with 40-watt bulbs do not seem to produce too much heat in general, but the grower should check this and place plants accordingly, at the same time providing good air circulation. When large numbers of tubes are used, as in a basement growing area, heat from the ballasts can be quite overpowering; they should be mounted outside of the plant room.

LIGHT CARTS

Various kinds of light stands and light carts are made commercially. There are little ones, one by two feet, which hold six to twelve plants and are topped by a bracket holding one or two (two is preferable) 24-inch 20-watt tubes. They make a pretty conversation piece for the living room, perhaps on a side table. There are also attractive stands in a multitude of shapes, designed more to be decorative than useful for very many plants, but fun to have. Larger stands or carts come with one, two, three, even up to six shelves, each with its own lights. Shelves are a bit over four feet long to accommodate 48-inch 40-watt tubes, and are usually 24 inches wide. Wider shelves are available. Fixtures are usually furnished with two 40-watt tubes for each two feet of shelf width (four tubes for a four-foot width), quite suitable for plants that are not light-demanding. For kinds that need a medium to high intensity it is better to have three or four 40-watt tubes to cover a two-foot shelf, or two of the HO ones. It is a good idea to have the shelves different distances apart to ac-

FIG. 11. *A light cart can offer various light intensities depending on the number of tubes per shelf, and whether plants are placed in the center or toward the ends of the tubes. The one shown here has fixtures holding two, three, and four 48-inch, 40-watt tubes, and plants are placed under them according to their light requirements. Some forty kinds of orchids are thriving on this cart.*

commodate plants of different heights, and some carts are made so that shelf height is adjustable.

The stands or carts may be placed where little or no natural light reaches them. However, since they are generally used in the living area of a home, it is often possible to locate them near a window so that they receive a little sun, and flowering may thus be improved. If the low-intensity 40-watt tubes are used, the more light-demanding plants will thrive on the shelves directly in front of the window, while those that need less light can be below or above window level.

Intensity is greatest close to the lights and drops off as the distance from them increases (see Table 1). It is generally stated that orchid plants need to be four to six inches below the regular 40-watt bulbs. However, since the light received by plants is related to their distance from the lamps, those with greater needs can be placed

TABLE 1. *Illumination in footcandles at various distances from two or four 40-watt standard cool-white fluorescent lamps:*

Distance from lamps (inches)	Two lamps (Used 200 hours)	Four lamps mounted 2 inches apart	
		Used 200 hours	New lamps
	Ft. c	Ft. c	Ft. c
1	1,100	1,600	1,800
2	860	1,400	1,600
3	680	1,300	1,400
4	570	1,100	1,300
5	500	940	1,150
6	420	820	1,000
7	360	720	900
8	330	660	830
9	300	600	780
10	280	560	720
11	260	510	660
12	240	480	600
18	130	320	420
24	100	190	260

(From *Yearbook of Agriculture*, U. S. Dept. of Agriculture, 1973)

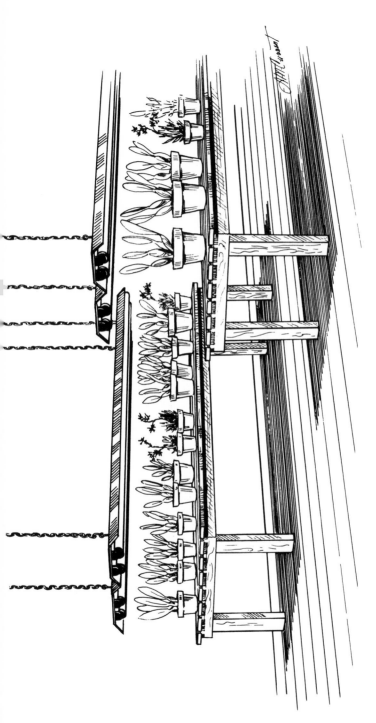

Fig. 12. Except that lights substitute for the sun, a basement growing area can be set up pretty much like a greenhouse. Benches can be of wood or pipe-frame. The bench top can be of slats, or it can be made to hold water to help with humidity. In the latter, plants should be set on racks or overturned pots to keep them above the water. Fluorescent tubes are in reflecting brackets suspended from chains so that they can be raised or lowered. The number of tubes per unit of bench area can be increased according to plant needs. Brackets holding four tubes close together are available.

close to them (short plants on overturned pots), and those that need less farther below. Light intensity also drops off toward the ends of the tubes, which means that light-demanding kinds should occupy the center position. An effort is being made to produce tubes that do not have this fault, and the G.E. Stay-Brite is a start in this direction. Flower spikes, even of very small plants, often grow quite tall, so that blooming plants have to be moved to the edge or end of the shelf to let the flowers extend outward.

The cart should not stand near a radiator or hot-air register, but where the house heat is conducted along the baseboard it may not be possible to keep the cart away from it. A fan or two should then be used to keep the air moving and bring cooler air to the plants. Ordinarily, the temperature varies from bottom to top, being cooler near the floor and warmer higher up, giving a chance to grow plants of different temperature requirements.

The shelves on ready-made carts have a built-up rim to catch and hold water, and a drain tap to remove excess water. If the one you order does not have racks on which to stand the plants, they can be made of redwood slats, galvanized hardware cloth, or expanded metal, or the plants can be placed on overturned pots.

Watering is, of course, managed according to the needs of the individual plants, and general treatment is the same as for window plants. A cool-mist humidifier with a blower will help if the humidity in the room is too low, and will also aid in keeping the air in motion.

BASEMENT GROWING AREAS

For a larger area than that furnished by a cart, a basement room is often chosen. Concrete walls and floors do not suffer from splashing water, spills, or overflows. Other rooms can be made to suit the purpose, however. It is desirable to paint the walls and ceiling white to reflect light. Benches can be made of redwood or ordinary lumber, or pipe-frames with wood or metal tops, or of second-

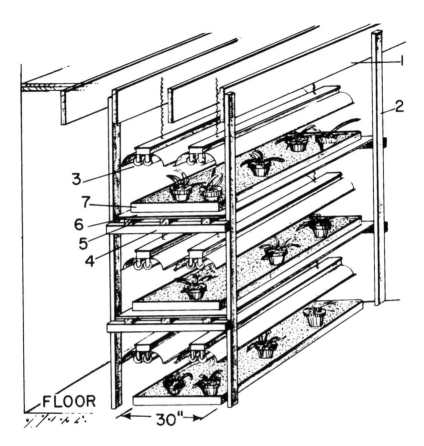

FIG. 13. *A tiered light setup. H-type frames resting on the floor are attached to the joists (1). Uprights are two-by-fours (2). Longitudinal supports (5) and cross bars (4) are two-by-twos, on which rest ¾-inch plywood platforms (6) of outdoor-type plywood. Metal trays (7) with turned-up sides, filled with gravel, can catch and hold water. Take care not to have plants stand in the water. Light fixtures (3) hang from chains for height adjustment. (Courtesy, GTE Sylvania, Inc.)*

hand tables. Regular greenhouse benches are available from dealers. If you wish, the benches may have built-up rims and be lined with heavy-duty plastic sheeting to hold water, or plants can be set on plastic trays. Neither setup is necessary if the humidity is high enough already.

The lights, in white reflectors, should be hung from the

ceiling by chains so that they can be raised or lowered. The number of regular 40-watt tubes to a fixture is determined by the kinds of orchids to be grown, for example two for a two-foot bench width for paphiopedilum and other low-light plants, three for phalaenopsis and those that require medium light, and four for cattleya, vanda, and others that need high intensity. The greater height of the basement ceiling, compared to shelves of light carts, makes such an area especially suitable for the HO and VHO lamps.

Regulating temperature is something each grower must do for himself. The lights will provide some heat, and may in fact raise the day temperature in a cool basement to just the right level, allowing the desirable drop of ten degrees at night. If additional heat is needed and cannot be supplied by the furnace, be sure that any gas or oil heater is perfectly vented, or else use electricity. As noted in the chapter on ailments, fumes from unvented heaters can cause flowers to be blasted.

A large number of tubes, particularly the high-output type, can produce excessive heat, and it may be necessary to install an exhaust fan to move air out into adjacent parts of the basement. The problem may be aggravated if the growing area has a low ceiling. If possible, install the ballasts of the tubes outside of the orchid room, thus eliminating one source of heat.

Basement areas often need to have fresh air brought in. During cold weather a window may be opened in an adjacent room for a short period each day, using a fan in the doorway of the growing area to draw the air in to the plants. Some growers open a window briefly in the immediate area itself, with a baffle to direct the air to the floor. During mild weather a window can be left open all the time.

If there is no separate room in the basement for the orchids, a corner can be curtained off with plastic to make a little "greenhouse," with fans to maintain air motion, and a heater and humidifier if necessary.

Watering and fertilizing follow the same general rules as for window plants, always related to the needs of the plants. They need more fertilizer with high-intensity light than with minimal light.

Indoor growers often notice that plants brought from a greenhouse undergo a shock when moved to a light setup. It appears that they have to make an adjustment to the new conditions, and that it sometimes takes a year or longer for them to regain their normal pace. Be patient, therefore, if your plants do not respond immediately. The opposite situation is also reported, that of plants that have been grown in poor natural light responding rapidly and favorably to artificial light.

DAY LENGTH

Artificial lighting has the advantage of being controllable; any desired day length is possible. A timer should be used to turn the lights on and off. They can be kept on for sixteen hours from spring through summer, or for that matter, all year round. The extra hours help to make up for intensity something less than that of sunlight. Seedlings especially benefit from the long hours, and the length of time to maturity can be shortened in this manner. When sixteen-hour days are given, plants may need more fertilizer to make robust, compact growth.

As mentioned earlier (this will be given in greater detail in the chapter on ailments), some orchids are sensitive to day length, refusing to bloom with long days. Therefore, if over a couple of years certain ones refuse to flower with sixteen-hour days, try moving them, after their growth is made up, to a place where they can be restricted to ten to twelve hours of light. This goes for those grown in the living area of the home as well. It would be a shame to deny the benefit of long days to plants that perform well with them, so you may wish to replace short-day kinds with others not so affected.

We do not mean to advocate sticking to sixteen hours of light. Many growers prefer to let the light period follow the natural day length of the season. We would say, however, that there is no use in letting plants suffer from the very short days of winter when you can so easily remedy the situation—twelve hours is a lot better than eight.

CHAPTER V

CATTLEYAS

The discovery of cattleyas was an accident, a fortunate happening that gave the world something new, and from which developed a far-reaching interest. The story goes that a Mr. Swainson, in 1818, was collecting mosses and lichens in the rain forests of Brazil. He gathered some heavy, flat-leaved plants to tie around his bundles. When these arrived in England, a Mr. William Cattley, an amateur plant enthusiast, saw the strange plants and took them home with him. In 1824 they flowered, and their magnificent blooms created a sensation in the horticultural world. They were turned over to Dr. Lindley, a renowned botanist, for identification. He found that they were orchids, but of a kind that had not been seen before, and he named a new genus to receive them. The new genus he called *Cattleya*, after the man who rescued them from oblivion, and he gave the species name *labiata* to this first member to be identified, descriptive of its most distinctive feature, its large ruffled lip.

This phenomenon of the plant world sent collectors hurrying to South America in search of more. Oddly enough, it was many years before any other plants of *Cattleya labiata* were found. Other species of *Cattleya* were discovered in Brazil, Colombia, Venezuela, Costa Rica, among them many that were similar to *Cattleya labiata* and equally lovely. Other orchids new to the eyes of man were also brought back, for which still more genera had to be created. It was truly an era of orchid discovery. Finally in 1891 a tremendous number of *Cattleya labiata* were found, so many that commercial florists of the day saw in them the possibility that we have seen come true—that cattleyas would become the foremost of all flowers for corsage use.

Cattleya labiata is still today one of the most desirable of the *Cattleya* species, both for growing and for use in hybridization. It is a radiant rosy-lavender, has a crisp, waxy substance, and an aristocratic posture on its stem. Its sepals are slightly pointed, its lip modest in size with a deep purple outer lobe bordered with lavender and a yellow or cream-colored throat streaked with purple. It flowers from late September into November.

The species that are similar to *C. labiata* are referred to as the "labiata group." The differences are so slight that some botanists would prefer to call them varieties of *C. labiata* rather than distinct species. However, they are generally treated as species, and are given as such in catalogs and hybrid registration lists. The members of the labiata group that are best known and with which you are likely to come in contact follow. *Cattleya trianaei* (Colombia) is somewhat lighter in color than *C. labiata* and has broader parts and a larger, more round lip. It flowers in mid-winter. Individual plants may flower for Christmas, but the majority of them come on in January. A species more dependable for Christmas is *C. percivaliana* (Venezuela), which is no longer grown commercially because of its small size, but which is richly colored and of interest to the collector. *C. mossiae* (Venezuela) is often called the Easter orchid because of its spring flowering season. It varies in coloring from pale blush to rich rose and has a lip veined and mottled with purple. In some the veining is sparse and not too attractive; in others so dense that the lip appears to be of almost a solid color. As *C. mossiae* finishes flowering *C. mendelii* comes into bloom, pale blush, sometimes almost white, with a patch of amethyst at the lower end of the lip. In June *C. gigas* (also named *C. warscewiczii*) flowers, the most showy of all the cattleyas. Its lip is very large in proportion to the rest of the flower, brilliant red-violet set off by two yellow eyes at the opening to the throat. There are true white forms of each of the above species. One other that is seldom seen in collections but which has been used in hybridization is the yellow *C. dowiana* (Costa Rica and Colombia). The flower shown in Fig. 2 is typical of the "labiata group."

The labiate species are less frequently grown now than they used to be, their hybrids having far surpassed them in overall quality and richness of color. However, good examples of the species are quite desirable, and a knowledge of them helps in understanding and appreciating the hybrids. Perhaps *C. mossiae* is the easiest to manage in the home. *C. labiata* must have short days to flower, hence will not bloom where lights are kept on in the evening. It contributes this habit to its hybrids.

There is another group of cattleyas, delightfully different from the labiates, more frequently grown as species. These are the bifoliates, so called because they have two or three leaves to the pseudobulb. Their flowers are in general smaller, more waxy, and have a wider range of colors, often decorated with spots. Their pseudobulbs are slender and rather canelike, and range in height from a few inches to two or more feet. *C. bicolor* is a tall one from Brazil, with flowers of olive or brown with a bright rose lip. The lip has no side lobes and completely exposes the column. *C. granulosa, C. leopoldii,* and *C. guttata,* all from Brazil, are medium-sized with spotted, waxy flowers in shades of green to brownish-purple. They have a fiddle-shaped lip, one that has a marked indentation between the front and side lobes. *C. skinneri* (national flower of Costa Rica), and *C. bowringiana* (British Honduras) are much alike, the latter a larger plant, and both give huge clusters of ten or more flowers of bright rose-

Fig. 14. Cattleya bicolor, *a green-brown flower with a red lip. It is one of the larger of the bifoliate species.*

violet, which in contrast to most of this group, are labiate in shape. C. *forbesii* (Brazil) is another with a tubular or labiate lip, a dainty plant a foot or so high with flowers in shades of cream, pink, and tan. C. *aurantiaca* (Mexico and Central America) rather resembles some of the laelias with its star-shaped, bright orange flowers. A true miniature is C. *aclandiae* (Brazil), barely three inches tall itself but with flowers three inches in diameter. They are creamy green with bold purple-brown spots, and a fat rose column set off by a pink lip with white, open side

Fɪɢ. 15. Cattleya walkerana *is a small plant with large, rather fleshy, deep rose-colored flowers.*

lobes. *C. luteola* is another miniature from Brazil, and has a cluster of two-inch yellow jonquil-like flowers. *C. walkerana* could be called the queen of bifoliates. It is a small plant from Brazil, with large velvety flowers of rich rose. It has the odd habit of making flower stems from the rhizome, alternating with the vegetative growths. This and *C. aclandiae* should be watered only occasionally between blooming and start of new growth.

Hybrids are made between the two groups, and in them one finds greater variety than in purely labiate hybrids.

FIG. 16. Cattleya forbesii *has dainty flowers of greenish tan with a cream and pink lip.*

Both are also hybridized with members of the related genera *Laelia, Brassavola, Epidendrum, Sophronitis,* and a few others. General culture is the same as for the species.

The growth and flowering cycle of cattleya species is typical of many kinds of orchids. The various phases can be followed in Figure 18. In late winter or early spring a bud, or "eye," at the base of the latest growth will swell and start to grow. The new growth, called the new lead, extends out horizontally for an inch or so and then curves upward. The horizontal section becomes an extension of the rhizome, while the upward-growing portion will produce the new pseudobulb and leaf, and subsequently the flowers. The developing growth is covered with clasping sheathing leaves which later on will dry to the texture of tissue paper. Soon the large, thick, true leaf emerges from the last sheathing leaf and rapidly expands. As the leaf opens, down within it can be seen a small, closed green envelope, the sheath, that protects the flower buds during their development. The developing growth and sheath

Fig. 17. Cattleya skinneri, *one of the bifoliate species, has clusters of many flowers on each stem. It makes a lovely early spring show of bright rose-violet blossoms.*

exude honey in thick droplets. While the leaf and pseudo-bulb are growing, they are tender and soft and can be easily broken. After they reach full size the leaf and pseudobulb become thick and tough, a process called hardening or maturing. The development of the complete growth takes from three to five months. Sometimes two buds will break from the same pseudobulb, giving the plant two leads instead of one, and often buds that have remained dormant for some time at the base of older

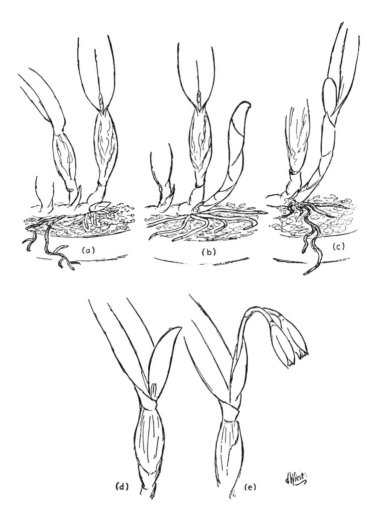

Fig. 18. *Growth cycle of a cattleya.* (a) A bud at the base of the lead begins to grow. At the same time new roots are formed from the base of the lead, and old roots make new branches. (b) The new growth lengthens and curves upward, covered by thin sheathing leaves that later become dry. The true leaf is just emerging. (c) The leaf and flower sheath are fully formed. (d) The pseudobulb becomes plump as it matures. Flower buds develop in the sheath. (e) Flower buds ready to open.

pseudobulbs will suddenly start to grow. Through the years a plant may develop many leads, and each lead increases the prospective number of flowers. Plants that habitually make many leads are very desirable.

The flower buds develop on a stem from the top of the pseudobulb and grow upward within the sheath. There may be from one to six buds, with two or three the average number. Their progress is slow at first, but as the buds become larger they grow more rapidly. They reach the tip of the sheath in from four to six weeks and then break through the sheath, grow rapidly larger and in about two weeks or more are ready to open. The developing buds are green up to this point—pure green for white flowers, tinged slightly with purple pigment in lavender ones. Drops of honey are formed by glands at the tips of the sepals and at their juncture with the stem.

As they prepare to open, the sepals lose the green coloring and take on the color the flower is to be. The opening flower is pale at first and the flower somewhat limp, but as it unfolds the color intensifies and the substance becomes heavier. It takes at the very least two full days to bring a flower to perfection; in some individual plants, four or five days. During the period of maturing the flower parts expand somewhat so that the flower when it is ready to cut is slightly larger than when it started to open. A flower must not be cut until it has attained its full color and substance. White flowers must have lost all tinge of green or cream. If a bloom is cut too soon, it will never acquire good color or substance, but will remain limp and pale and fade after two or three days. Cattleyas should keep in water at room temperature for a week or more, and longer under refrigeration, in water, at about 45°F. The flowers last longer on the plant, two weeks at least, and up to six weeks for individuals of exceptional substance.

Cattleya blooms are usually fragrant while they remain on the plant. The fragrance does not last long after the flowers are cut, however, so that to those who have

known them only in the florist shop the fact that they are
fragrant comes as a surprise.

A wave of root activity accompanies either the flush of
new growth each season or the starting of flower buds.
One pattern in cattleyas, which is found in many other
kinds, is for new roots to form just as a new lead is
starting. Another pattern is for new roots to start just as
the flower buds begin to develop. The roots become evident as little bumps on the underside of the basal curve of
the pseudobulb. Soon the green tips of the roots break
through the dry covering tissues. As the roots grow longer,
the surface behind the green growing tip becomes white
with the developing velamen. The roots are extremely
brittle and are easily broken, and they are also tempting
to slugs and snails. Injury of the growing tip causes the
root to stop growing in length. A root that has grown to
about five or six inches in length will form branch roots if
its growing tip is injured, and older roots will branch in
successive years.

In Figure 18 the development of new roots can be followed along with the developing growth. In Figure 19(a)
new roots are forming along with the starting flower buds;
(b) is included to show still a third pattern, illustrated by
an oncidium, in which new roots form from the young
growth itself when it is about one-fourth or one-third
along. Once in a while a cattleya growth will form roots
when partially developed.

An orchid plant does not have nearly as extensive a
root system as our garden plants. The roots are rather
thick, and, even though an old plant may appear to have a
tremendous number of roots, the total absorptive surface
cannot compare to the root system of other kinds, which
have thousands of fibrous feeder roots and millions of
root hairs. The epiphytic orchids do not have root hairs.
The relatively scanty root system must be well cared for if
the plant is to thrive, and this creates the great need for
caution in watering and for the insurance of good aeration
and drainage. Let the potting medium become almost dry
between waterings, then water thoroughly. Give fertilizer

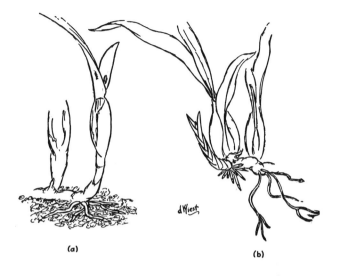

FIG. 19. *(a) Some cattleyas form new roots at the time flower buds develop, rather than when new growth starts. (b) Another habit of root formation, shown by many kinds other than cattleyas, is illustrated here by an oncidium. Roots form from the new growth as it develops, rather than from the mature growth.*

at every other watering as described on page 26.

Cattleya species have certain little idiosyncrasies in the timing of the various phases of their growth and flowering cycle. Knowing what to expect of a plant helps in caring for it through the year. The patterns shown by the kinds we describe here will also show up in the hybrids, so that a brief summary will not only be of value in growing the species but in pointing out what general kinds of habits to watch for in hybrids, for instance the habit of holding the green sheath for many months before flowering, or of making roots along with flower buds instead of with new growth, or the habit of the sheath to dry before buds appear in it.

C. *gigas* goes through the cycle more rapidly than any other. It starts growth in January and develops it rapidly. Flower buds start pushing up in the sheath almost before it has fully emerged from the leaf, and without any pause for the maturation of the growth. The flowers open in June or July. After flowering, new roots form.

C. labiata starts its new growth and new roots together in January or February, and these are well along by March, with the growth mature by July. Flower buds start up in the sheath in early September and the flowers open in October or November. The sheath is double, a sheath within a sheath, and this characteristic shows up in the hybrids. However, other kinds occasionally produce a double sheath even when there is no *C. labiata* in their makeup.

C. trianaei starts its new growth in March and matures in about August or September. Then, just as the flower buds start up in the sheath in November it produces its new roots. The flowers open in about January, depending on the habit of the individual plant.

C. mossiae spreads its complete cycle a bit by having a late spring flowering time. It starts new growth in May or June, not long after flowering. The growth does not mature until about October. Now the plant waits for some months before any further activity is evident. Growers who do not know this habit often become impatient, thinking the plant will never give flowers, and the habit shows up in many hybrids. Then in January or February new roots form, and soon thereafter the flower buds start up in the sheath, to open in April or May. *C. mendelii* follows this same pattern.

C. skinneri makes its new roots along with new growth starting in about April. Its growths are mature by the end of the summer, and during the autumn the sheaths turn brown and become quite dry. Flower buds form in the dry sheaths in the winter, sometime during January or February, and open in about two months.

CHAPTER VI

OTHER KINDS TO GROW

Many of the orchids we shall describe can be grown in more than one temperature situation, and some genera have species that like one situation just as well as another, so we shall present them to you as genera and give their requirements individually or as groups. As mentioned previously, a light cart may have different temperatures depending on the distance from the floor; a window arrangement may offer a cooler temperature on the side nearest the glass than on the side farthest into the room; and under lights, whether in a basement or a cart, it is warmer closer to the lights. All situations allow plants to be moved up or down, back or forward, to find the right place.

EPIDENDRUM, ENCYCLIA, LAELIA, SOPHRONITIS, BRASSAVOLA

This group of cattleya relatives comprises a thousand species, many of which have been crossed with each other and with cattleyas to make attractive hybrids. The species themselves are delightful. Those we give here all like intermediate temperatures.

EPIDENDRUM AND ENCYCLIA. *Epidendrum* and *Encyclia* are often put together under *Epidendrum,* and you may very likely find them so in catalogs; the species name will be the same, but the generic name will be *Epidendrum.* Many epidendrums have slender, leafy stems; some are too tall for indoor growing, but there are some smaller that you would enjoy. *Epi. difforme,* whose stems are six inches tall with six to eight spatula-shaped leaves, has a cluster of fragrant, waxy, one-inch greenish-white flowers in late summer. *Epi. coriifolium,* a few inches taller, has narrow, very thick leaves, and a stem of fleshy flowers from pale to dark green, sometimes verging on black, in mid-winter. *Epi. ciliare* is a great favorite, its fragrant white flowers as delicate as feathers. It has slender pseudo-bulbs, and flowers any time from fall to spring. These three do well in medium light, watered like cattleyas.

A delightful group in *Encyclia* are the shell orchids, those which have a shell-shaped lip held uppermost, and petals and sepals spread below it. *Encyc. fragrans* and *radiata* have a cream-colored lip striped with pink or violet, while the lip of *Encyc. cochleata* is greenish with purple stripes on the front, nearly black on the back. Its green petals and sepals stream downward, giving it the appearance of a little marine creature. All have pseudo-bulbs, and vary in height from six to fifteen inches. *Encyc. mariae* is a dainty plant, six to eight inches tall, and has three-inch green flowers with a huge, wavy, white lip. *Encyc. atropurpurea* (*cordigera*) is a heavy plant with conical pseudobulbs and foot-long leaves. Its magnificent fragrant flowers, three to four inches long, have mahogany-colored sepals and petals that curve forward gracefully at the tip, and a large rose-colored lip; one form has a white lip. The blossoms are produced on stems about eighteen inches long holding about a dozen blooms. A well-known little Florida native is *Encyc. tampense,* which has acorn-sized pseudobulbs, slender little leaves, and spikes of one-and-a-half-inch reddish flowers. All of these like medium to bright light, and are watered like cattleyas.

FIG. 20. Epidendrum difforme, *a delicate and lovely small species with reed-like stems and waxy, greenish-white flowers.*

FIG. 21. Encyclia cochleata, *one of the "shell" orchids. There are several regional forms, not all of which have such long, streaming petals and sepals, but all are attractive.*

FIG. 22. Encyclia atropurpurea (cordigera), *a popular and showy species, with mahogany-colored petals and sepals and a rose or white lip. It is delightfully fragrant.*

FIG. 23. Encyclia tampense, *native to Florida, has delicate stems of small perky reddish flowers.*

Fɪɢ. 24. Laelia harpophylla *is one of the many species with clusters of star-shaped flowers. It is a soft orange, while others range from pink to yellow and red.*

Lᴀᴇʟɪᴀ. *Laelia* includes plants that run from the large *L. autumnalis* and *anceps,* which have yard-long spikes bearing clusters of four- to five-inch bright rose-purple flowers, and can be accommodated only in a spacious area, to some charming miniatures. The big ones must have bright light and they require a decided dry rest after their mid-winter flowering. A miniature is *L. lundii,* very easy to grow and only four inches tall, with slender stems and narrow, quill-like leaves. Its exquisite inch-and-a-half

FIG. 25. A *near-miniature cattleya hybrid*, Cattleya luteola × C. aurantiaca, *is but one of many small hybrids for a small space. It is bright yellow. The plant is a nice illustration of growth from the seedling stage to maturity.*

Fɪɢ. 26. Sophronitis cernua *has bright-eyed orange flowers that show up even among large-flowered neighbors.*

lavender flowers emerge just as the leaf tips appear from the new growth in mid-winter. The blossoms are tiny editions of a cattleya, with a wee ruffled lip. It needs to be kept rather damp except for a brief early fall rest, and can be grown in either low or medium light.

In between these two sizes come many other species, among which is an array of Brazilians with clusters of delightful brightly colored star-shaped flowers. The plants have tough, slender, tapering pseudobulbs and equally tough, rather rough leaves. Their two- to three-inch flowers are produced atop twelve- to eighteen-inch stems, mostly during the winter. *L. harpophylla* is a soft, glowing orange, *L. flava* a bright yellow, and *L. milleri* fire-engine red. These three must have bright light, and a dry rest after maturing their growth and until flower buds appear. All laelias are watered like cattleyas but are given a definite dry rest.

Some of the hybrids among the small-flowered laelias and epidendrums and the large and small cattleyas give compact plants with shorter flower stems bearing clusters of up to ten bright flowers. They are most rewarding for small areas.

SOPHRONITIS. *Sophronitis* is a genus of small plants and bright flowers. *S. coccinea* is difficult to grow, or rather to keep growing from year to year, but you might like to try it. It likes rather cool temperatures, constant dampness, and medium light. It is only four inches tall yet has flowers two to three inches across. You should know it because its red to orange flowers have been the progenitors of many lovely red hybrids made with *Cattleya* and *Laelia*, giving flowers that range from two to five inches in diameter. A cross between it and *Epi. radicans*, a tall-growing reed-stem plant, produced the popular *Epiphronitis* Veitchii, a small reed-stem with clusters of bright red flowers, very free-flowering. *Soph. cernua* is much easier to grow than *coccinea*, and enjoys intermediate temperatures and medium light. It is a rambling yet compact plant, with tiny fat pseudobulbs and leaves, and clusters of half-inch bright-eyed orange flowers in mid-winter, sometimes at other times of the year as well. It does best on a slab of tree fern or cork bark, wetted once a day.

BRASSAVOLA. Two species of *Brassavola* are equally well known, but for different reasons. *B. digbyana* is a cattleya-like plant with huge greenish-white flowers; its unusually large lip is beautifully fringed. This species has been crossed many times with *Cattleya* to make *Brasso-cattleya* hybrids. The fringe is not always, in fact rather seldom, carried on in succeeding generations, but the lip size is, and so is the fragrance of the flower. The species requires medium to bright light, with a moderate rest (infrequent waterings) after its late summer flowering and until new growth begins. *B. nodosa* is a lovely plant, with slender white flowers that are fragrant at night, for which reason it is affectionately called "lady of the night." It is grown like any cattleya.

ONCIDIUM, ODONTOGLOSSUM, BRASSIA, MILTONIA

Here is another group comprising several hundred species. Shapes and colors occur in great variety, some quite fantastic. Many will interbreed, and charming hybrids have been made among them.

ONCIDIUM. Best known of the oncidiums are the "dancing dolls," which produce showers of one- to two-inch bright yellow flowers that have small sepals and petals and a huge flaring lip. Of these, *Onc. ampliatum* has turtle-like pseudobulbs and broad, flat leaves, and its flowers are a bit more stiff than the others. *Onc. verrucosum* var. *rogersii* has fluted oval pseudobulbs; its lip is often two inches wide, a veritable flowing skirt. *Onc. flexuosum* is a smaller, very dainty "doll," with a somewhat climbing habit that makes it suitable for growing on cork bark or tree fern. These three all need bright light, intermediate temperatures, and cattleya watering.

Some other oncidiums have little flowers without the exaggerated lip. A few are too large for house plants. Of fair size are *Onc. baueri* and *ensatum*, which have dense sprays of small yellow and brown flowers. Smaller plants are *Onc. cabagre, obryzatum,* and *uniflorum,* also yellow and brown; *Onc. ornithorhynchum,* which has pendent sprays of small rose-lilac flowers with a huge yellow crest; and *Onc. cheirophorum,* a near-miniature with dense sprays of little bird-like yellow flowers. These like medium to bright light, intermediate temperatures, and watering as for cattleyas.

Fig. 27. *A small plant can have a wealth of flowers, as shown by* Oncidium obryzatum, *whose blossoms are yellow and brown.*

A group called the "mule ear" or "burro ear" oncidiums is characterized by fleshy leaves shaped exactly like the ears of those animals. They are without pseudobulbs. Too large for a plant cart, but suitable for a spacious area under bright lights, are *Onc. carthagenense* and *cavendishianum,* which have tall spikes of fleshy flowers, the former white and purple, the latter yellow-green. Two species with similar leaves but much abbreviated pseudobulbs are *Onc. splendidum,* which has a tall branched stem of three-inch flowers with brown forward-curving petals and sepals barred with yellow and a huge

FIG. 28. Oncidium verrucosum *var.* rogersii *produces a veritable ballet of "dancing dolls" dressed in bright yellow.*

flaring yellow lip, and Onc. *microchilum*, which bears an upright stem of small brown flowers. All four like intermediate temperatures and bright light.

Two lovely oncidiums for cool temperatures are Onc. *incurvum*, a medium-sized plant with long branched sprays of delicate one-inch flowers, white barred with pink, and Onc. *phalaenopsis*, a small plant with a short stem of five or six dainty one-inch flowers that are white, spotted with rose or violet. A very striking cool-growing one with big round brown flowers is Onc. *forbesii*, and two quite like it which prefer intermediate temperatures are Onc. *gardneri* and *crispum*. Again, bright light is necessary, and watering as for cattleyas.

FIG. 29. Oncidium ornithorhynchum *has pendent sprays of small rose-lilac flowers with a huge yellow crest.*

FIG. 30. Oncidium phalaenopsis *is a delightful small species, white, with rose markings, and sweetly fragrant.*

Fig. 31. *Large round brown flowers trimmed with yellow make*
Oncidium forbesii *a striking species. Shown here are but two branches
of a many-branched inflorescence.*

ODONTOGLOSSUM. Among odontoglossums, *Odont. grande* is famous as the "tiger orchid" for its four- to five-inch brown flowers, boldly striped with yellow. It will thrive either in cool or intermediate temperatures, and medium or bright light. It must have a period of lessened water during winter, beginning after it ends its fall flowering. Quite different is the dainty *Odont. pulchellum,* a slender plant that gives arching stems of eight to ten one-inch flowers, waxy, white, and very fragrant, in midwinter. It thrives in low light and needs to be kept damp all year. For cool temperature and medium light, there is the charming miniature *Odont. rossii,* with flowers two to three inches in diameter, of an odd combination of brown sepals and petals (sometimes almost rust color) and a

Fig. 32. The "tiger orchid," Odontoglossum grande, has bold yellow and brown flowers.

white or pink lip. It prefers to be constantly damp. *Odont. pendulum* is one of the loveliest of the genus. A medium-sized plant, it produces a pendent stem of three-inch fragrant flowers that are white, shaded delicately with pink. It must be absolutely dry during winter. In the spring new growth will appear and from its tip, before the leaves emerge, the flower stem grows out rapidly. Do not water it until the flowering stem is a couple of inches long. It likes cool temperatures and medium light.

BRASSIA. Brassias are fantastic orchids; their flowers are extended in length by tails on the petals and sepals, earning them the nickname of "spider orchids." The flow-

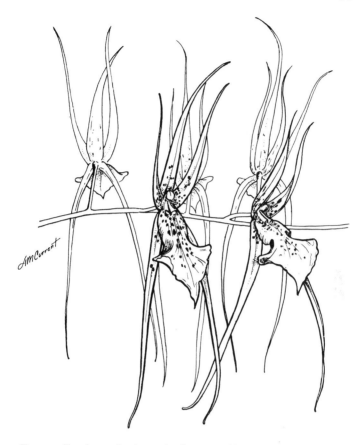

Fɪɢ. 33. *For fantastic shape the brassias add a note of charm. This one is* Brassia verrucosa, *with flowers in tones of green.*

ers stand in two neat rows on the curving stem, all facing in the same direction, and come in shades of green and brown with a speckled lip of a lighter green. *Brs. verrucosa* and *gireoudiana* form a stiff phalanx with their tails absolutely straight. *Brs. longissima (antherotes)* has the longest tails of all, exceeding ten inches on the lateral sepals and somewhat wavy. *Brs. caudata* is smaller and also has wavy tails. All are easy to grow in medium light, intermediate temperatures, and with no dry rest.

Fig. 34. *Miltonias, the "pansy orchids," have a serene beauty. This one is* Miltonia roezlii, *white with purple and yellow markings.*

MILTONIA. Miltonias have large, delicately fragrant, sweetly rounded flowers resembling pansies. Their plant proportions are dainty, their flowers are produced two to four to a stem, and all have butterfly markings in the center. For cool-intermediate temperatures *Milt. vexillaria* and *roezlii* are most rewarding. The former makes large plants with many leads and has pink flowers; the latter does not branch out so readily and has white flowers. *Milt. regnellii* and *spectabilis* prefer intermediate temperatures. The former is white shaded with purple; the latter is also white and purple, but it has a variety *moreliana* that is all rose-violet. Many hybrids are available and are more commonly grown than the species. All like low to medium light and constant dampness, but must never be allowed to become soggy as they are vulnerable to rot.

DENDROBIUM

This is another huge genus, with every imaginable size and shape of plant and flower, and too many different habits to attempt to describe here. We will suggest a couple, however, and ask you to consult books and dealers to find others to try. *Dend. phalaenopsis* (neither this nor the oncidium of the same name is related to the genus *Phalaenopsis*) and its myriad hybrids are easy-going and have arching stems of two- to four-inch flowers in shades of pale to deep violet. Since its cane-like pseudobulbs can grow quite tall, better allow it plenty of space; fifteen inches is a short plant, eighteen inches average. It makes new growth in the spring, and pauses when that is complete, at which time it should have less frequent waterings. It then blooms from both new and old canes, during which time it is again given normal watering. After flowering it should be kept absolutely dry in the pot, with occasional misting of the foliage, until the new growth has appeared and *begun to make its own roots.* Another kind, one to watch for because it is such an unusual one and so well adapted to indoor growing, is *Dend. lawesii* from New Guinea. It will gradually come on the market but is uncommon in this country now. It has leafy fifteen-inch pendent canes that flower once before losing their leaves, and then bloom on the naked canes year after year. The flowers are rather tubular, a bit over an inch long, and come in dense clusters at the nodes of the canes. They are bright red or rose, and last for from three to five months. It likes medium light and intermediate temperatures, and must be kept damp.

FIG. 35. Dendrobium phalaenopsis *flowers from both the new and the old canes, with blossoms varying from pale to deep rose-purple.*

FIG. 36. *Varying in color from pale lavender with a dark lip to rich deep violet,* Dendrobium phalaenopsis *has flat, wide-open, velvety flowers.*

Fig. 37. *Clusters of fiery red blossoms are produced year after year on the same canes of* Dendrobium lawesii. *The group shown here consists of clusters from several adjacent nodes. Remains of stems of other clusters can be seen above the flowers.*

CYMBIDIUM

The big cymbidiums, called "standard," are rather a gamble for indoor growing. The HO and VHO lights offer a greater possibility of success with them now, for they are very light-demanding. They do require low night temperature, close to 50°. It is said that they will do with higher night temperatures if they have a definite drop between day and night of more than the usual ten degrees. However that may be, success is more likely with the cooler nights. One big problem for indoor growers is their size. They are tall, two to three feet in height, and they quickly become massive, wide-spreading plants. One can take up to four square feet. The spikes ascend to three feet or more. The flowers are waxy, very long-lasting, popular for corsages, and range in color from white to yellow, green, pink, and red, usually with darker spots in the lip. They respond to being grown outdoors during the summer, and where they can stay out from May through September, they have a chance to make their growth and initiate flower spikes before being brought in. The flowers open best with cool temperatures—they can be blasted by too great heat. A wide choice of hybrids is available.

The small, recently developed so-called miniature and poly-min hybrids prefer warmer temperatures and can be grown along with cattleyas, under the same light conditions. The plants are smaller, but not true miniatures; they can be eighteen inches tall or more. The spikes are sometimes taller than that, more often not, and the flowers are small versions of the large flowers albeit often more brightly marked. Even these take up quite a lot of space, but less than their big brothers.

All cymbidiums require constant dampness at the roots, which are fleshy. They can be grown in bark or tree fern, but special potting mixes commercially made are better. Their worst enemy is red spider.

FIG. 38. *The standard (large, cool-growing) cymbidiums are not truly house plants, but can be grown where they can spend the summer outdoors, and be given a cool, bright spot indoors for flowering. Shown here is a typical hybrid. Not shown is the so-called miniature or poly-min type that is more amenable to indoor culture. Insets: left, vegetative shoot; right, flower spike starting.*

FIG. 39. A *typical hybrid of the large-flowered, cool-growing type of cymbidium. The waxy flowers keep two or three months on the plant and six weeks or more when cut.*

CHAPTER VII

MORE KINDS TO GROW

PAPHIOPEDILUM

These are the lady-slippers, or slipper orchids, extremely popular, easy to grow, and ideal for indoor growing because they are undemanding of light. Their lip has become modified into a pouch, which suggested their name. In the waxy, long-lasting flower, the large dorsal sepal stands on top like a banner, the petals extend sideways, sometimes downward, and the lateral sepals are fused together in a single structure that hides behind the lip. Colors go all the way from white to red, with the majority in shades of brown and green. Few are of a single color, most are striped or tinted with other hues. Many hybrids are available, but all of the species are desirable and many are popularly grown. The plants are of medium size or smaller so that they fit well on a light cart, and most will do beautifully in either low or medium light. Delightful ones for either cool or intermediate temperatures are *Paph. spicerianum*, green with a large turret-shaped dorsal sepal; *Paph. fairrieanum*, greenish, striped with purple, with a wavy-edged dorsal sepal and petals that curve gracefully downward; and *Paph. insigne*, yellow-green with brown spots. For intermediate or warm temperatures there is a charming almost dwarf species, *Paph. venustum*, in shades of green and brown,

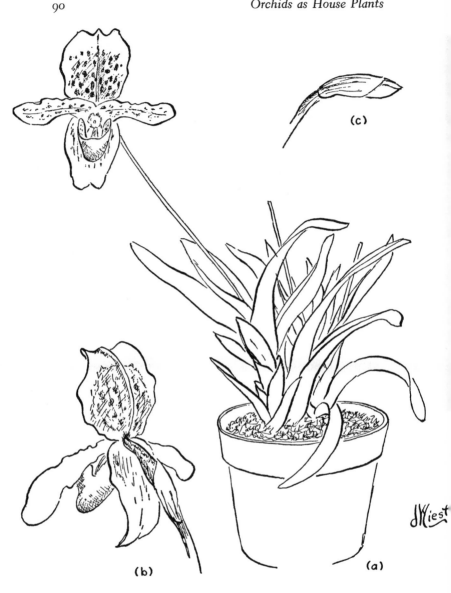

FIG. 40. Paphiopedilum insigne, *a popular species. (a) Plant in flower showing new growth coming from its base. (b) View of flower from the back, showing the large dorsal sepal and below it the fused lateral sepals. (c) Flower bud emerging from its sheath.*

FIG. 41. Paphiopedilum fairrieanum, *a delightful medium-size species, and but one of the many kinds that can be grown successfully in the home.*

and two lovely and quite similar hybrids, *Paph.* Maudiae, and the larger *Paph.* Clair de Lune, both of which have ice-green flowers whose dorsal sepal is white, striped with green. All like to be constantly damp, and should be given fertilizer only once a month. They are terrestrials and require a more loamy, fibrous potting medium than bark, which can be obtained from some orchid dealers. Plants can be grown on with several leads. When one is to be divided, simply break it apart with your fingers, making units of one or two leaf fans together with the new growth.

Fig. 42. A *catasetum is a fascinating conversation piece.* Catasetum integerrimum *belongs to the group with an upright hood-shaped lip. Within the hood can be seen the active trigger that, when touched, releases the mechanism that shoots the pollinarium.*

CATASETUM AND CYCNOCHES

CATASETUM. If you like flowers that "do" something, you will enjoy *Catasetum*, which shoots the pollinia when a trigger is touched. There are species that have separately male and female flowers, although female ones are seldom produced in cultivation. Some have an upright hood for a lip, within which stand the whip-like triggers (one functional and one inactive), and others that have the lip lowermost with the triggers hanging down from the column. There are also species with perfect flowers, both sexes in the same flower. Most kinds are deciduous—they make a lovely fan of thin many-veined leaves through the summer, and these fall after growth is mature. During or after leaf fall, flower spikes are produced from the base of the pseudobulb. After blooming, the plants should be kept dry until new growth starts in the spring. Kinds you might like to try are *Ctsm. integerrimum*, with green flowers tinged with brown, *Ctsm. viridiflavum*, yellow-green, both of which have the hood-shaped lip uppermost, and *Ctsm. pileatum*, a lovely large yellow one, whose dish-shaped lip is held downward. The female flowers of this group are so much alike that it is difficult to tell their species. They have the hood-like lip uppermost, no triggers, and a short, stubby column. Of the perfect type, nothing is prettier than *Ctsm. roseum*, pink, and *Ctsm. scurra*, green-white, which have one-inch globular flowers and a fringed lip. They have a little sensitive "beak" that springs the pollinia. All of these species like bright light and intermediate temperatures, and should be watered like cattleyas when in growth or flowering. Spray them regularly for spider mites.

CYCNOCHES. Everyone loves the "swan" orchid, commonly sold as *Cyc. chlorochilon*. Experts tell us that this name refers to a rather rarely seen species, and that the one we know is really *Cyc. ventricosum* var. *warscewiczii*. The plants resemble those of *Catasetum*, are deciduous, and require the same care. They have very waxy four-inch chartreuse flowers, with a white lip shaped like the body of a swan. The slender, arching column, capped by the knobby anther, carries the resemblance further. Its delicious fragrance fills the room. Plants usually produce just male flowers, but occasionally female ones appear, or flowers bearing both sexes, and these differ in appearance from the male flowers only by the shorter, more stubby

FIG. 43. *The "swan orchid"* (Cycnoches chlorochilon), *as it is pop-ularly called, loses its leaves as the flowers develop. The chartreuse-and-white flowers are extremely fragrant.*

column. Flowering occurs in mid-winter, during or after leaf-fall, from the upper nodes of the pseudobulb. Other species of *Cycnoches* are charming as well, among them *Cyc. aureum* and *egertonianum,* in which the petals and sepals are thin and curly, and the lip edged with filaments. The female flowers of these resemble the flowers of the "swan."

MASDEVALLIA

Masdevallia belongs to a group of genera that includes *Pleurothallis, Stelis, Restrepia,* and others, but it is the most beautiful and colorful. The showy part of the flower is formed by the sepals, which are usually fused at their base into a broad or narrow tube, while their tips are prolonged into short or long tails. The petals and lip are much reduced in size and nestle in the bottom of the tube. The plants themselves are pretty, with paddle-shaped leaves on short petioles (no pseudobulbs), and the flower stems are produced from the base of these. A striking species is *Mas. coccinea* with three-inch short-tailed flowers in glorious shades of rose, red, and, less commonly, yellow or pale lavender. A dainty one is *Mas. tovarensis,* which has three white flowers to a stem, with somewhat longer tails and a total length of three inches. A huge, furry, ferocious-looking one with long tails is *Mas. chimaera,* about eight or nine inches long, quite open, and with a bobbling, fluted lip. This one is very sensitive to dry air, and wilts if the humidity drops. All of these require cool temperatures, low light, and constant dampness. For the intermediate range, a flashy one is *Mas. militaris,* about the size of *coccinea,* red with orange stripes. Commercial dealers offer an assortment of species from which you can find other types.

Relatives of *Masdevallia* offer some charming small-flowered things. *Pleurothallis* has a number of plant types, one of which has heart-shaped leaves and tiny flowers emerging from the base of the "heart," which make them pretty pot plants. Some others have paddle-shaped leaves similar to *Masdevallia,* and give many-flowered stems of yellow or purple bells. *Stelis* has plants much like *Masdevallia,* and has upright stems of three-pointed stars; the flowers are one-fourth inch in diameter, some smaller, the conspicuous part formed by the sepals, while the lip and

FIG. 44. *Masdevallias are lovely indoor plants for a cool location. They multiply rapidly into perfect bouquets. Shown here is* Masdevallia coccinea, *which has flowers in shades of rose and red.*

petals are mere swellings in the center. *Restrepia* is, again, similar in plant form, and has flowers produced at the back of the leaves. They have large fused lateral sepals, and filamentous petals and dorsal sepal. Flowers are

FIG. 45. *A charming miniature species is* Stelis argentata, *which grows equally well with cool or intermediate kinds.*

about one-half to one inch long, barely rising above the leaves. Some members of these three genera like cool, some intermediate temperatures. All can be grown in an in-between situation. They like low light and constant moisture in the pot.

PHALAENOPSIS, VANDA, ASCOCENTRUM, AND OTHER MONOPODIALS

PHALAENOPSIS. This beautiful monopodial genus is ideal for an orchid case in a south window, and it also does marvelously well under lights. Although many other kinds of orchids can be grown in a case, phalaenopsis flowers are so showy and so long-lasting that they make a breathtaking display for many, many months. The flowers of the big hybrids, particularly the white ones, stay fresh on the plant for from three to five months, and more buds open at the end of the graceful spike as the first ones fade. After flowering, cut off the section that produced blossoms, and a branch may form from a lower node. Blooming periods of individual plants may overlap so that the case is seldom without flowers. They need a temperature not lower than 60°, preferably 65° at night. In a south window the course of the sun matches their seasonal needs very well. From spring to fall they need less light as this is their growing season; they make a new leaf or two and new roots. At this time the sun is overhead so that no direct light enters the window. Toward fall, the summer leaf is mature and the plant is ready to initiate flower spikes, at which time its need for brighter light is supplied by the southward-turning sun. Through the winter the brighter light helps form flowers of large size and heavy substance. It is necessary to pull a thin curtain or a double layer of cheesecloth across the window from about mid-morning to mid-afternoon if the sun warms the case too much and threatens to burn the leaves. Most plants will initiate their spikes under the conditions prevailing in the case, but if they do not, putting them in a cooler place, temperature just below 60°, for two or three weeks may spur their development.

The large hybrids have round flat flowers from three to four inches across, of a velvety texture, and in colors ranging from white to shades of yellow, pink, or rose. Some are speckled with yellow or pink. They have two or

Fig. 46. *Phalaenopsis plants remain in flower for many months, with sprays of ethereal blossoms in white, pink, or yellow. The large-flowered hybrids or species make a beautiful display during most of the winter.*

three pairs of broad flat leaves, six to twelve inches or more long. Since they grow slowly and remain of short stature, a mature plant takes up about the same amount of space throughout its lifetime. There are lovely species, but you are more likely to find hybrids listed in catalogs, and would enjoy almost any you see offered.

Small species come in many colors, some with round

Fig. 47. *The serene beauty of the large white phalaenopsis hybrids is unequaled.*

flowers, some with star-shaped ones. These and the delightful little hybrids create a nice contrast to the large-flowered ones. A beautiful miniature is *Phal. equestris,* whose one-inch pink flowers open three or four at a time over many months. Another is *Phal. lueddemanniana,* which has very waxy two-inch flowers in shades of cream to deep rose.

Watering depends somewhat on the climate in which they are grown. Some Florida growers say to let them dry out between waterings, but the humidity outdoors in Flor-

FIG. 48. *A seedling phalaenopsis hybrid usually flowers while quite small, giving only a few flowers but with the promise of great numbers to come.*

ida may be quite different from that in a home. We feel that they do best when they have fairly constant moisture at the roots, coupled with humid air. They should be given fertilizer at every other watering. As the lower leaves fall, the base of the stem becomes naked and deteriorates. Roots on this old part die off. Plants should be repotted when the lower inch or inch-and-a-half has reached this state, choosing a time when a new leaf and new roots are forming. Remove the plant from the old pot, break off the lower, dead, part of the stem, which will carry its dead roots with it. Trim back any broken roots or dead ends. Nestle the bottom end of the stem and live roots into the fresh medium, and firm the material around them. Bark (medium to coarse grade), tree fern, or osmunda fiber are good potting materials.

VANDA. These majestic monopodial plants, with their stems of flat round colorful flowers, really need bright light and lots of space. They should have full sun in a window, or a four-tube fixture of 40-watt fluorescent lights, or, better, the high-output kind. Granted that some will grow with less light, they tend to become rather spindly and do not flower vigorously. They will do well with intermediate temperature, somewhat better with warm. They can be grown in the same room with *Phalaenopsis*, provided the light requirements of each is met. You may like to investigate the species available, but may have best results with hybrids, of which there is a wide array to choose from.

ASCOCENTRUM. *Ascocentrum* is a genus of small vanda-like plants with bright flowers. Two popular species are *Asco. curvifolium*, with dense sprays of half-inch red-orange to purple flowers, and *Asco. miniatum*, very much like it and with bright orange blossoms. The chief interest in these is, however, the delightful hybrids made with *Vanda*, called *Ascocenda*, which are moderate-size plants, more suitable than vandas for small areas, and eye-catching with their bright one- to two-inch round flowers. They need bright light, warm temperatures, and plenty of water and humidity.

OTHER MONOPODIALS. Dozens of other monopodial orchids are available, requiring intermediate to warm temperatures—lovely things from the Orient, Madagascar, and Africa. There are *Aerides* such as *fieldingii*, with a dense spray of fragrant pink flowers, and *quinquevulnerum*, with sprays of white flowers tipped with bright purple; *Aeranthes*, a genus that has green flowers of fantastic shape on thread-like stems, among them *ramosus*;

Fig. 49. Vanda *Rothschildiana, a famous blue hybrid, flowers several times a year.*

Aerangis, which has white star-shaped flowers with long spurs, one of which is *compta*; and *Angraecum.* In *Angraecum* there are huge plants such as *sesquipedale,* a big star-shaped flower with a ten-inch spur, and *eburneum,* whose flowers have a somewhat shell-shaped lip and a short spur. These might not be recommended for indoor growing because of their size, but the hybrid between them, *Angraecum* Veitchii, is smaller, and quite suitable for a medium to bright situation. A delightful miniature is *Angraecum compactum,* which has spurred white waxy flowers about an inch-and-a-half across.

OTHER GENERA

There are many additional possibilities for indoor growing. In fact, the only real limitation is your own desire and willingness to search out and try other things. The genera *Gongora, Cochleanthes, Chondrorhyncha, Lycaste, Coelogyne, Dendrochilum, Maxillaria, Bulbophyllum, Dichaea, Trichopilia, Ludisia* (one of the "jewel orchids"), and many others offer beautiful species of easy culture.

CHAPTER VIII

POTTING
MATURE PLANTS

The general method used for potting cattleyas can be applied to other orchids, with only slight modifications. Where such modifications are necessary, they will be described.

An orchid needs repotting either when it has outgrown its pot, that is, when more than one growth has gone over the edge of the pot, or when the medium has become broken down. But if the plant is in good health and the medium is good and firm (not crumbly or not shrunken so that the plant wobbles in it), it may not need repotting for three or four years.

All orchids should be repotted during their period of active root formation, preferably just as the new roots are starting, so that they will grow into the fresh medium. There is no point in repotting a plant at all unless you give it a chance to reestablish itself quickly. Hence we do not advise shifting a plant when its growing season is over and it is not able to make new roots for several months. A plant that is disturbed at such a time is forced to spend a long period without functioning roots and may be set back considerably. In those kinds that form new roots from the newly developing growth, the time to repot is when the growth is two or three inches tall and new roots are expected in a few weeks. In kinds which form new

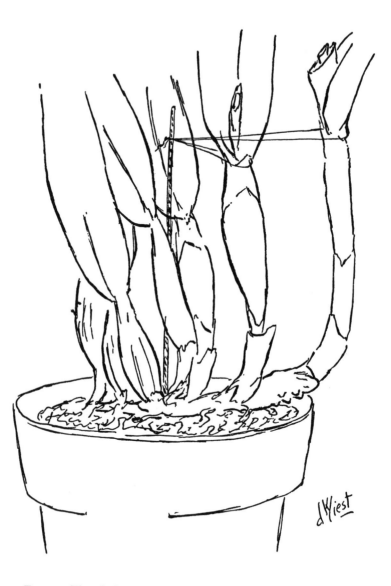

FIG. 50. *The ideal time to pot a cattleya (or any orchid) is when new roots are beginning to form. In this cattleya plant the new roots are evident as little bumps on the underside of the lead.*

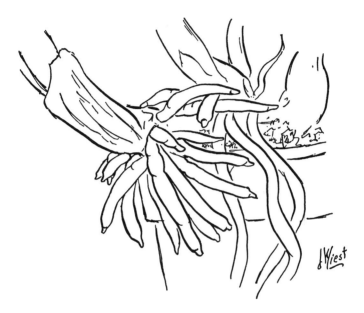

FIG. 51. *New roots too far along to be handled without injury.*

roots from the mature lead at about the time the "eye" begins to swell, the time to repot is just when those new roots are evident as little "bumps" and before they have begun to grow rapidly. When the new roots are lengthening they are easily injured, and so we do not like to handle a plant with the new roots from one-fourth inch to about six inches. We shall give more information about this in a moment.

As the new roots start from the lead, the wave of activity spreads to older roots, and these send out many branches. Old roots of which the tips have been injured will send out new green tips all along their length. They thus assist in making new roots, expanding the root system year after year, and for this reason it pays to take

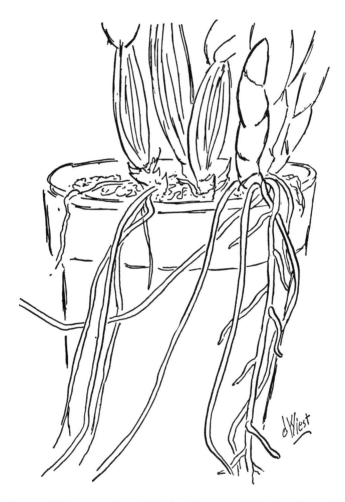

Fig. 52. *New roots about six inches long, at which time they will branch if the tips are broken. Plants can be potted at this stage.*

good care of them. When repotting we are careful to leave clean stubs of the old roots, which quickly give rise to branches and, together with the new roots from the lead, furnish a wealth of active roots.

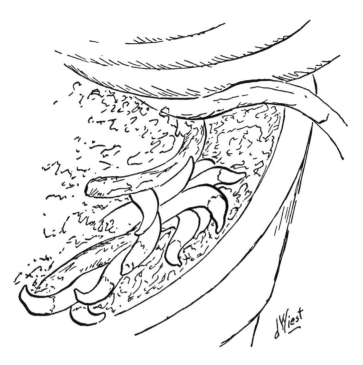

FIG. 53. *Cut stubs of roots, both old and new, give rise to branch roots that quickly reestablish the plant.*

While the old roots branch freely from a short stub, new roots do not seem to have this capacity for some time. If they are injured while still quite short, their activity for that season comes to an end. However, if they are allowed to grow until they are six inches or so in length and then should be injured, they will send out branch roots. This gives us a second chance to repot a cattleya whose new roots get started before we can get the job done. Also, it is handy for plants that make new roots while flowering, for instead of trying to shift them with buds that could be damaged, we can wait until flowering is over.

DIVIDING PLANTS

Some growers like to keep plants small, keeping them down to five- and six-inch pots at the most. Commercial growers often do this with their selling stock, for a one-lead plant is priced lower than one with several leads, and this size is easier to pack. They are also more uniform as to space and watering. Other growers, ourselves included, find that a plant with many leads can take less space than the same plant divided into smaller sections. For instance, a plant of five pseudobulbs with a single lead may stretch across a five-inch pot, while a plant with three leads spreading out fanwise would also fit a five-inch pot. A plant in an eight-inch pot can have eight or nine leads and will produce more flowers than the number of single lead plants that could occupy the same space. We move plants on into larger pots until they become unwieldy, and then, of course, they have to be divided.

Some plants habitually break many leads; others give rise to only one lead a year. Even plants that give many leads do not develop all the buds that are capable of producing new growths. Many buds remain dormant at the nodes of older parts of the rhizome. Removing the lead growth, as when a plant is divided, stimulates one or more buds on the older part to develop. Thus when a plant is cut in two, the younger part with the lead growth goes on as before, while the "backbulbs" or older part, now deprived of a growing end, will develop new lead growths from dormant buds. There is sometimes a question as to whether to divide a plant with several leads, but there is no question when it comes to a one-lead plant of eight or nine pseudobulbs. If the latter is simply potted again, the chances are that it will go on giving only one lead, so that you get no increase in flower production for an ever larger pot. By dividing it you get two plants that will flower.

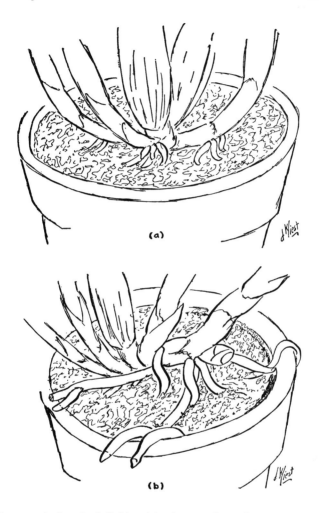

FIG. 54. *A three-lead division (a) takes up about the same amount of space as a one-lead division (b).*

A lead division consisting of four or five strong pseudo-bulbs with leaves should flower on the first growth after division. A backbulb division of several pseudobulbs with leaves may flower on its first new growth, or may wait for the second year. But a weak backbulb division, one that

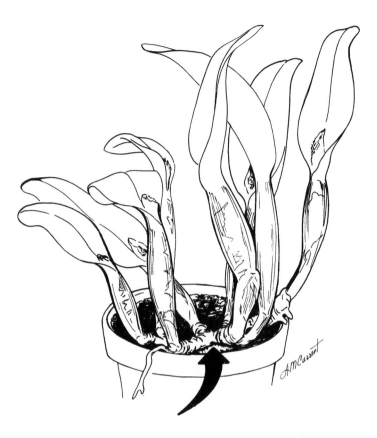

Fig. 55. *A one-lead plant, to be divided as shown by the arrow.*

has only one or two pseudobulbs, often without leaves, will make but a small growth its first year, one a little larger the second, and may wait for the third year to flower. For this reason, unless they are from a valuable plant, we ordinarily do not save the oldest pseudobulbs.

Since plants do not conform to any one pattern, little problems come up as to where to make a division. Try to make each division a strong plant. In dividing a one-lead plant, keep three or four pseudobulbs together for the

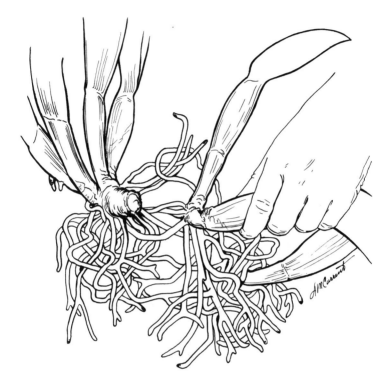

Fig. 56. *The plant, removed from the pot and cut in two. Roots will be trimmed back to two-inch stubs.*

front division, making the cut through the rhizome behind the third or fourth pseudobulb. Use your own judgment about saving the back part. In dividing a plant with many leads, it is not necessary to break it up completely into one-lead plants. Some leads may have developed so recently that to separate them would make divisions of only two pseudobulbs. Rather, try to keep them in neat groups, perhaps two leads on one division, or even three, making the cut behind the pseudobulbs from which they arose so that they are joined as one plant. When repotting a plant that is not large enough to be divided, it may be wise to remove the oldest pseudobulb just to economize space. When a plant has recently matured from seedling stage, we often remove the small pseudobulbs remaining from this stage as they do not contribute much to the plant. Sometimes this enables you to put it back into the same size pot again.

POTTING EQUIPMENT

You will need an array of pots in various sizes, depending on the size of plants you are growing, a sharp knife, pruning shears, galvanized steel stakes, soft but non-stretchy string, labels, and perhaps a metal potting stick. Either clay or plastic pots may be used; the latter retain moisture longer than the former, but are lighter, easier to clean and disinfect, and are less expensive.

Fir bark, Douglas fir bark, and chopped tree fern are excellent media for all kinds of orchids except some terrestrials, the barks being more commonly used in this country. The barks come in grades according to the size of the pieces—a very fine grade for tiny seedlings, a grade ranging from one-fourth to one-half inch for larger plants, and on up to a very coarse one- to one-and-a-half-inch size for very large plants. Tree fern also comes in grades according to the length of the fibers.

All tools must be sterilized after work on each plant so as not to spread disease, particularly virus, from one plant to another. Tools are best flamed; an alcohol lamp, a Bunsen burner, or a small blowtorch may be used for the purpose. Stakes and pots that are to be reused must also be sterilized. Stakes can be heated in the oven for ten minutes at 250° F. Pots should be washed clean and then be soaked in Clorox solution, one part to ten of water, or in Physan, one tablespoon to one-and-one-half gallons of water. We should add that even when cutting flowers or pruning off leaves, the blade used should be sterilized before moving on to another plant. We like to use cheap razor blades, depositing each one in a container after use on a plant, and these are later sterilized by boiling for twenty minutes.

POTTING

Drainage material should be placed in the bottom of the pot, partly to prevent the hole or holes from becoming clogged, and partly to allow air to circulate to the roots. Many growers like to enlarge drainage holes before use. Drainage material may be coarse gravel, lightweight aggregate, or broken pieces of old pots (sterilized, of course).

Choose a pot to allow for two years' growth, estimated by the space between pseudobulbs, or, for kinds without pseudobulbs, by the overall size and needs of the plant. Thoroughly soak the pot in which the plant is growing so as to loosen the roots from the sides and allow it to be knocked out easily. If roots still cling, run a sterilized knife around the inside of the pot. With the plant out of the pot, shake off the old medium, removing it by hand if necessary. You do not have to pick off every piece, just see that most of it is removed. Cut off all dead roots, and trim healthy ones back to a two-inch stub. If a cluster of young roots can be saved by not disturbing the material around them, let them remain intact in that portion of the medium. Pull off loose dry sheathing leaves from the pseudobulbs (not from the rhizome). Divide the plant if necessary, or perhaps remove only the oldest pseudobulbs.

Bark may be used wet or dry. Your hands will become less stained if it is dry, but damp bark is easier to firm in the pot. Tree fern should be soaked and drained to make the fibers more pliable.

To pot a front division or an intact plant, hold it within the prepared pot with the old end back against the side. Pour in some bark, fingering it down among the roots.

FIG. 57. *Potting the lead division. Hold the plant so that the older end is against the side of the pot, allowing space in front of the growing end. Fill in with bark, keeping the plant at the level shown, about one-half inch below the rim.*

Thump the pot several times on the bench to settle it, and then pour in some more. Firm it as you go along, using your fingers or the potting stick. Bring the final level of bark to about a half-inch below the rim, with the rhizome of the plant lying in a trench at the surface. Push a galvanized stake into the bark clear to the bottom of the pot,

FIG. 58. *Press the bark down firmly with thumbs or a potting stick, so that it is quite solid. Allow the top side of the rhizome to be just above bark level.*

and tie each pseudobulb to it individually. If the plant should have few roots to hold it, so that it is wobbly, press a piece of stake or stiff wire, cut just longer than the diameter of the pot, down across the rhizome. The pressure against the inside will hold the wire in place, and it will hold down the rhizome.

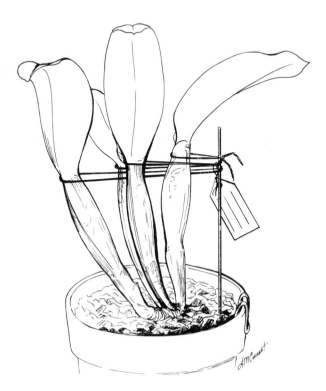

FIG. 59. *Stake and tie the plant. Be sure to add a label.*

When using tree fern, place a handful over the drainage material. Then, with the plant in your hand, tuck some under and among the roots to make a kind of ball. Holding this in the pot, tuck more tree fern under and around it, firming it solidly, and finally fill the pot up to the rim and firm this with the potting stick.

Label the plant as soon as you are finished with it—it is easy to forget which is which when you have done several.

To pot monopodials in general, see the directions given for *Phalaenopsis* in Chapter VII. For taller monopodials, e.g. *Vanda*, the top section of the plant can be cut off and set down into a potful of fresh medium. These tall plants usually make aerial roots along the stem. Even one such root can give a division a new start, and other roots will form. Therefore, cut the plant just below one of the upper roots. The old part of the plant can be left in its pot, or can be repotted, and perhaps it will eventually make a side branch that can be removed and potted in its turn. It may be several years before the side branch reaches a size to be potted independently.

Plants such as *Masdevallia*, and others with growths clustered close together, usually require a pot small for their size. This is also true for many dendrobiums, whose stems grow at close intervals. As you handle plants of different growth patterns, you will become accustomed to judging what pot size they require. It never does to put a small plant in a large pot—the center of the medium is likely to stay too wet for its good. Along this line, a plant that is not doing well will sometimes improve if put in a smaller pot.

Back divisions are potted in the same way as front ones, with the younger end allowed space to make new growth. You can often encourage leftover pieces, single pseudobulbs or old backbulbs, to break dormant buds by putting them in a polyethylene bag with a couple of handfuls of damp medium. Tie the bag at the top and set it upright in a warm place with low light. When new roots begin to show, pot it up. The bag technique is also useful for starting newly collected plants if they arrive without sign of new growth or in a dried condition.

After being potted, plants should be given a little less light than usual. The stems and foliage should be misted frequently. They will be inactive, or less active, until the new roots are long enough to absorb sufficient water and minerals. Misting helps replace water lost through evaporation. Do not give water in the pot until the roots are two or three inches long, but include the surface of the medium in the misting to keep it damp for the developing roots. You will be well repaid for resisting the temptation to water too soon, for in these few weeks the old root stubs, which might rot if kept wet, will heal and send out branch roots. When the plant is established, put it back in its usual place and on its normal schedule.

Sometimes a plant needs to be put in a larger pot because of unusually rapid growth, yet does not need to be removed from the medium. Simply knock it out, fit it into a larger pot, and fill in with additional bark or tree fern. Plants are often shipped "out of pot" to save postage. These can be treated in the same way, being fitted into the size pot they obviously were in, or moved on into a larger one.

CORK-BARK AND TREE-FERN SLABS

Some orchids just do not like pots but prefer to be fastened to a mount around which their roots can twine and thus have extra free aeration. Some kinds can be grown either in pots or on mounts. Often the habit of a plant dictates which system is better. Those whose pseudobulbs grow upward from each other, each one higher than the one before, and those that make masses of roots that grow out of the pot (vandas and phalaenopsis excepted) often do better mounted. The mount does not have to be cork or tree fern, it can be a slab of oak bark or other hardwood, or just a piece of wood, or, for small plants, a cut section of a hardwood branch. The latter are most attractive laced with the roots of a small plant.

To attach a plant, place a shallow layer of sphagnum moss or osmunda fiber on the surface and wrap it around with thin plastic-covered wire or nylon fishing line. Then position the plant and wind the wire or line around its roots and between its growths. Repeat with other plants if they are to dwell on the same mount. Fasten a wire to one end, with which to hang the finished product. Some species do best with their roots completely exposed, and for these no moss or fiber is necessary—just fasten them to the bare surface. The wire or fishing line can be cut away after the roots have taken hold, but by then may be so well hidden that it need not be removed.

CHAPTER IX

CARE OF
SEEDLINGS

There is something about growing a plant all the way from an early stage that gives a special feeling of achievement. There is also an aura of mystery surrounding a seedling that increases as it approaches maturity, for not until it flowers will you know the secret it has held during its development. It is an experience everyone should have.

The earliest stages of seedling growth are easy to manage in the house, for they require a soft light and a warm, humid environment. Large numbers of young seedlings can be accommodated in a small space, so that if you plan to have a greenhouse within a year or so, you can get a head start by growing some seedlings indoors. By the time they are outgrowing a two-and-a-half-inch pot—in other words, by the time they are half grown—they will have the same light and temperature requirements as adult plants. If a greenhouse is not in your future, or at least some expansion of growing space, it is not wise to acquire very many seedlings.

An orchid seed pod is started on its way by placing the pollinia from one flower on the stigma of another. The pod takes from six months to a year to ripen, depending on the kind. When the seed is ripe, the pod is harvested and the seed stored in a dry, cool place, often in a desiccator in a refrigerator. The seed is almost powdery, just

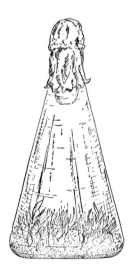

FIG. 60. A *flask of seedlings.*

discernible with the naked eye as small white or brown
elongated particles. In nature the seed is wind-borne,
wafted from the pod and scattered by air currents. Of the
hundreds of thousands of seeds in one pod, only a few
will find just the right conditions for germination, such as
a damp pocket of humus shaded by other plants. The tiny
seed does not store much food, and so the developing
seedling depends on fungi to release sugar and nutrients
for its use.

In cultivation sugar and nutrients must be provided for
the use of the seedlings. Dr. Lewis Knudson of Cornell
University, in 1922, developed the method of germinating
the seed now in use. The seed is disinfected to kill any
mold spores and is then sown in sterile flasks or bottles on
an agar jelly containing the necessary mineral salts and
sugar. After the seed is sown, the flasks are stoppered to
prevent the entrance of mold spores, and the stopper is
covered with foil or polyethylene film to protect it from
contamination. The flask acts as a little greenhouse, in

which the seedlings develop without disturbance or injury.*

The seedlings remain in the flasks for about a year, at which time they are ready to be transferred to pots.

COMMUNITY POTS

When the seedlings are about half an inch tall (some kinds become larger in the flask), they are transferred to community pots. Some growers put them in small flats. Twenty to thirty plants can be put in one pot, the advantage of which is that they can be kept uniformly watered.

In order to remove seedlings from the flask, a small amount of water at about 70°F is poured in and swirled around, and then water and seedlings are poured into a shallow bowl. Two or three repetitions should remove most of the plants. The last few which may be buried in the agar can be lifted out with a dinner knife. Any agar clinging to the roots will dissolve away in the water. The process of potting is shown in Figure 61. Fine-grade seedling bark is used.

Community pots require a humid atmosphere and a night temperature of 60° to 65°F, and should not be allowed to dry out. They can be put in an orchid case in which you are growing warm orchids, placed so that they are well shaded by other plants. Or they can be grown in a small case, if you have one, or a "growing box" made from a fruit lug with a glass lid. Community seedlings require about 200 footcandles of light when they are just out of the flask (about the same light required for the flasks themselves), which can be increased in a month or two to 300 footcandles, and in another month to 400 footcandles. The growing box or seedling case may be set near a window, with appropriate shade—a piece of mus-

---

* For details on growing and sowing seed and the care of flasks, and for information on hybrids and hybridization, see *Home Orchid Growing*, by Rebecca T. Northen, 3rd revised edition, 1970, Van Nostrand Reinhold Co., New York.

Fig. 61. *Transplanting to a community pot. The seedlings removed from the flask float in a bowl of water. Handle them gently with tweezers or fingers, putting each in place and pressing the fine bark against its roots.*

lin or two or three thicknesses of cheesecloth over the glass lid. Or the pots may be set under a low-light fixture consisting perhaps of a single 20-watt tube with provision for ample humidity.

A seedling case must have some ventilation, for even though the little plants like a high humidity they cannot compete with molds and algae likely to grow under too damp conditions. The glass lid should be propped up a crack, or the top part of the front and back of the box should be lowered to allow air movement. A slight opening will allow exchange of air without lowering the hu-

Fig. 62. *A growing box for small seedlings made from a fruit lug, with a piece of glass for a lid. A piece of muslin or cheesecloth is used for shading if the box is to go into a window, but may not be necessary under low-intensity artificial light. Note that the front and back sides of the box are lower than the ends, to give ventilation when the lid is down. These plants are just out of community pots. The larger ones have been put into individual pots, the smaller ones back in a community.*

midity too much. We would rather have this ventilation and spray the plants once a day than to keep the air saturated.

The community pots should be watered often enough to keep the medium damp, but in the humid atmosphere of the box or case, and with the daily misting, they may not have to be watered very often. Give fertilizer every two weeks.

The tiny seedlings are susceptible to damping off. To prevent this, water the pots when they are first planted with Benlate (Benomyl 50-W), Natriphene fungicide, or Anti-Damp (8-quinolinol sulphate) made up according to directions, and repeat at two-month intervals.

INDIVIDUAL POTS

The plants remain in community pots for about eight months. By that time you will notice that some have become quite sturdy plants, while others are still fairly small. The larger ones are ready for individual two-and-a-half-inch pots, while the smaller ones should spend a few more months in communities.

Gently lift the seedlings from the community and separate their roots. Some roots may be broken, but the plants will soon replace them. A one-fourth-inch grade of bark is available for seedlings of this stage. Using it, and with the little pots prepared with drainage material, simply place the seedling in the pot and fill in with the bark. A fine grade of tree fern can also be used. Prepare fresh community pots for those not quite large enough for individual ones, and plant them exactly as if they had just come from a flask, although, to be sure, they are larger.

The individual pots should go into a growing box with the light intensity at first the same as before, or under the single tube mentioned above. After a few months the light can gradually be increased to 600–800 f.c. in a window, or the pots can be moved to a two-tube fixture. They still need to be kept damp in the pot, and to have fertilizer every two weeks. Regardless of the species, they will grow faster if the nights are between 60° and 65°F. A sixteen-hour day also accelerates growth.

After they have spent a year in these pots, they should have made a considerable increase in size. Cattleyas should have made a plump little pseudobulb and a leaf three to four inches tall; paphiopedilum leaves should be two or three inches tall; phalaenopsis leaves should be two inches long. If you do not care to try the younger seedlings, this is the age at which seedlings are most easy to care for. They are sturdy, they have passed safely through the more tender phases, and it will not be too long before some of them bloom.

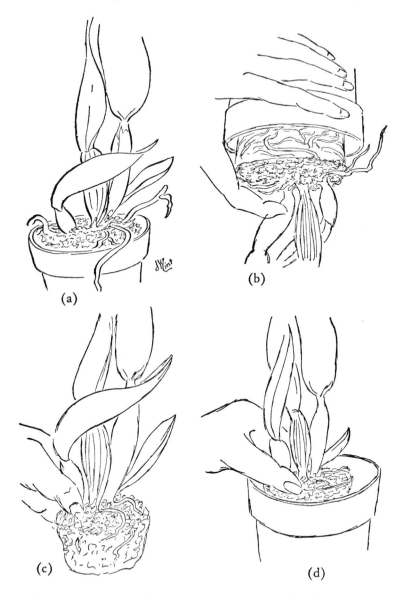

FIG. 63. Moving a seedling on into a larger pot. (a) The plant to be repotted. (b) Knocking it out of the pot. (c) The ball of roots is left intact. (d) Fitting it to its new pot. Simply fill in with bark.

READY TO FLOWER

When the seedlings outgrow their two-and-a-half-inch pots they should go into four-inch pots. An occasional very large seedling may merit a five-inch one. This time they are potted as mature plants, for they should flower in these pots. It is not necessary to disturb the roots, and they may be moved whenever their growth merits it. After they have been repotted, do not water them for two weeks, but mist the foliage daily. They can now all have the same light conditions as the adult members of their kind, as well as the temperatures preferred by the grown-ups.

The time required from flask to flowering size varies with the kind and with the speed of growth. Some plants are naturally more vigorous and make more rapid progress than others. If the average grower flowers cattleyas in four or five years from the flask, he is doing a good job.

The first flowering of a seedling may be just as vigorous as that of a mature plant, but often the flowers are somewhat smaller and fewer in number than they will be the second time. Cattleyas sometimes make a sheath as they approach maturity but fail to flower in it. When this happens you can expect the next growth to flower. Phalaenopsis may produce only three or four flowers on their first spike, while the second may have many more. If the first flowers of a seedling are large and handsome, you can know you have a good plant. If they are small, yet of good color, shape, and substance, the chances are that they will be better the next time. If they are poorly shaped or colored, the chances are not so good that they will improve the next time, but it is worth waiting to see, for sometimes increase in size and vigor of the plant will produce larger, heavier flowers.

CHAPTER X

AILMENTS
AND PROBLEMS

When orchids are given healthy environmental conditions, few problems arise. Most orchids are quite tough and fairly resistant to diseases and the depredations of the usual pests. However, it is better to know what to look for than to be unprepared, and occasional ailments occur even in the best-managed collection. The following are the kinds of trouble generally experienced, although not necessarily of frequent occurrence; possible causes and prevention are described.

TEMPERATURE AND DAY LENGTH

If the rest of your plants flower, indicating that your general culture is good, but one or two fail, it may be that these particular ones are more sensitive than the others to night temperature. For instance, an intermediate kind may refuse to set flower buds unless it has a night temperature of 55° for two months or so after the growths have matured. You might try moving the plant to a spot with cooler night temperature. Some others may fail to flower if the night temperature is too cool. A little experimenting with individual plants that are temperamental may give results. Plants may become dehydrated or otherwise weakened by too high temperatures, either night or day or both.

Day length influences the initiation of flower buds in

many plants, including some orchids, or it may control the development of the flower buds that have been initiated previously. In *Cattleya labiata,* for example, flower buds are actually formed by cells at the tip of the pseudobulb during the development of the pseudobulb in early summer. These minute buds are visible only with the aid of the microscope. They remain microscopic all during the summer and start to grow up in the sheath only as autumn comes on. The factor that brings on the growth of the flower buds is the short day length of autumn, and *C. labiata* is therefore known as a "short-day" species. Growers who wish to have *C. labiata* in bloom for a certain date can control its flowering by giving it artificially long days until two months before flowers are desired. In practical application, this is done by spacing 100-watt bulbs ten feet apart in the greenhouse and turning them on at sundown for as many hours as necessary to bring the total number of light hours to 16. Lighting must be begun well before the buds start pushing up in the sheath. As soon as the artificial lighting is discontinued, and the plants allowed to have the normally short days of fall or winter, the buds begin to grow, to open in about two months. This species has been held from flowering by long days for as much as a year. Many of its hybrids follow the same habit and are known as "controllable" hybrids.

Many kinds are prevented from initiating or developing flower buds by long days. On the other hand, some will do so only with long days. Each species has to be studied by itself, a long and tedious process, and, although much has been accomplished, we still do not know the habits of many kinds.

In a greenhouse, the day length follows the pattern of the seasons, but in a home the occupants make the days artificially long by the use of electric lights. Plants placed somewhat away from the light may not be affected, but those that stand near the lights may be prevented from flowering. It does not take a very high light intensity to make the difference between day and night for a plant. If some of your indoor plants fail to flower, it may be that they are "short-day" plants. It would be worth experimenting with these by giving them short days as soon as the growth has matured. Perhaps you can move them into a room that is not used during the evening, or devise some other means of giving them ten hours of light and fourteen hours of darkness. We tried this on a hybrid that had not flowered in two series of sheaths. Two months after short-day treatment was begun, the plant was in flower on growths made both years. Once the buds are well up in the sheath a plant can be returned to the long-day situation, for long days will not cause the already growing buds to stop.

FAILURE TO FLOWER
AND POOR FLOWER SUBSTANCE

Any environmental condition that impairs the health of a plant may be the cause of failure to flower, such as insufficient light, improper temperatures, or overwatering. A "blind" growth is one that does not flower. Failure of the growth to form a sheath may mean that it is not going to flower, but buds often come without a sheath.

When a sheath becomes dry, it may mean that flowers will not come. However, buds can come in a dry sheath, even as much as a year later. Do not cut off the dry sheath unless, when buds form, they seem to have difficulty pushing up in it. Then cut it off just above the tops of the buds. Sometimes in hybrids the sheath may be too small for the buds, or too long, or too tough. Sheath character is not always inherited to match the length of flower stem or size of buds. Keep an eye on the developing buds, and cut off the sheath's top or open it if the flower stems are becoming bent double in it or the flowers are too crowded. Some plants form a double sheath, which usually causes no trouble, but, again, if the buds have difficulty, open it.

Buds occasionally die in a normal sheath. We think the problem is a nutritional one in some cases. Either the plant is not strong enough to support the flowers, or some condition impairs the health of the plant while the buds are developing. Such conditions can be high temperatures (night or day), overwatering, or poor light. We have seen it happen with a seedling flowering for the first time, with a recently divided plant, with one heavily shaded by other plants, and with plants kept in an orchid case that is allowed to become too hot and steamy. Occasionally it happens on a plant flowering on many leads, where one lead may fail to develop its flowers.

Blasting of buds and flowers is a rare occurrence, but once in a while buds ready to open will turn pink or brown and fall off. They may have become too cold, for instance if they touch the cold window glass, or too hot if they have stood in direct sun.

Poor substance—that is, flowers that are thin and fade before they should—may be an inherited fault or may be due to poor growing conditions. If a plant gives thin flowers year after year, failing to improve when culture is corrected, there is probably nothing to do but discard it. However, a plant that normally gives good substance may make thin flowers when some cultural condition is wrong. Our experience with indoor plants is that their flowers are of equal quality to those grown in a greenhouse.

SEPAL WILT, FREAKS, YELLOW LEAVES, LIGHT BURN

Sepal Wilt. An ailment called "sepal wilt" affects a good many kinds of orchids, but is best known as affecting cattleyas. The bud develops normally, but sometimes before it has a chance to open it is blasted, or if it opens, the sepals turn papery within a day or two and soon thereafter become brown or black at the tips. In the former situation, the whole flower is ruined; in the latter, the petals and lip last in good shape for about their normal length of time, but the flower is spoiled by the dried sepals.

It has been known for some twenty years that ethylene gas in the air causes sepal wilt. It may be a component of air pollution, or it may come from leakage of fumes from incompletely vented oil or gas heaters, breaks in vent pipes, even from faulty pilot lights on household appliances. It takes only an extremely minute amount to do the damage, for cattleyas as little as one part to 300,000,000 to 500,000,000 parts of air. This is far less than the amount needed to cause tomato plants to fold their leaves, or carnation flowers to become "sleepy." Ethylene gas is used to ripen fruit that has been picked green—it functions as an agent to mature or age the fruit. In orchids, it brings about premature aging. Other components in polluted air may also damage flowers.

Sepal wilt can come on suddenly, and cease as suddenly. Buds that have not reached a stage to be vulnerable will open normally when the gas disappears from the air. Flowers already open at the time may not be affected. Even on the same plant, some flowers may be damaged while others that open later (or had opened earlier) escape. There is not much that can be done about industrial gases or pollution from a nearby highway (except move away, as some commercial growers have done), but possible sources in the home can and should be carefully checked.

Kinds in addition to cattleyas that can be affected include some species or hybrids of *Laelia, Catasetum, Stanhopea, Cycnoches, Vanda, Cymbidium,* and *Maxillaria.* It seems odd that in some genera not all species are affected —an affected one can be standing right beside one that shows no symptoms.

FREAKS. Freaks can show up in any kind of plant, and orchids are not immune. A pseudobulb with a sheath and no leaf, a flower with no lip or with the wrong number of parts, a column fused to the lip, sepals fused together, petals that have some lip structure—any of these, or any other strange "mistakes," happen once in a while on perfectly normal plants. A freak flower can even occur on a stem with normal flowers. Some growers call such deformed flowers "cripples," while scientists call them "anomalies." They usually do not appear again on the same plant and are nothing to worry about. Nor are they of any value. Their cause is some accident in the development of a particular growth or a particular flower. It would require a deep-seated change in the genes of the plant itself (a mutation) in order for the freak to be repeated. An individual plant can have a quirk in its genetic makeup that causes crippled flowers to appear rather regularly, but such a plant may give normal flowers sometimes and deformed flowers at other times. Some of the yellow cattleya hybrids are notorious for this. A plant that gives normal flowers more often than deformed ones may be worth keeping, but should never be used as a parent.

YELLOW LEAVES. If the leaves of a plant turn yellow, the first thing to look for is overwatering. The yellow leaves in this case are a symptom of starvation because waterlogged roots can absorb neither water nor minerals. Another cause may be too much light, which can destroy chlorophyll and bleach the leaves. A third cause may be cold, but in this case the leaves become rather mottled with yellow or yellow-green.

LIGHT BURN. A light burn is actually a heat effect. The tissues are killed by being raised to too high a temperature by light absorption. The burned area remains localized and eventually dries. If it occurs at the very tip of the leaf, it may be cut off after it has dried to improve the looks of the plant. If it is centrally located, do not cut off the leaf, for any living parts of the leaf can still make food and contribute to the strength of the plant.

DISEASES

Diseases of plants are caused by viruses, bacteria, and fungi. As in any class of living things, some diseases are fatal, and some are not; some can be alleviated, and some, thus far, have no cure. Plants, like people, may show individual resistance to certain diseases, or some may be more susceptible.

Diseases caused by bacteria and fungi show up first as watery spots which become sunken and brown as the tissues in the area die. In contrast to a light burn, the spots usually enlarge or become more numerous. A disease may start at the tip of the leaf, gradually spreading down the length of the leaf. Or it may start in the rhizome, killing off pseudobulbs and leaves as it progresses. A few spots may appear and then become arrested if the plant is resistant or if their spread is controlled. Soft, succulent growth is more easily attacked than hard growth.

Bacteria multiply within the plant tissues and come to the surface in oozing droplets (often too small to be seen by the naked eye). Fungi send their cobweb-like body into the tissues, while reproductive spores develop on the surface. The diseases are spread by transfer of the droplets or spores to the surface of healthy plants. Insects, or human hands, or tools, or drops of water splashing from one plant to another can effect the transfer. If the surface on which the organisms land is wet, the bacteria multiply and the fungus spores germinate, to enter the leaf tissues by such openings as leaf pores, insect punctures, or wounds. *Water on the leaf or sheath or pseudobulb is a partner to the spread of disease.* Allowing the foliage to dry off after watering or misting, and ventilating to assure an exchange of air and prevention of stagnation, are important steps in disease prevention. Sanitation, cleaning up fallen flowers and plant parts that can harbor disease organisms, and control of insects and weeds that harbor insects, are other preventive measures.

General use of a fungicide is a final preventive measure, although it may not be necessary if the foregoing precautions are taken. It is indicated if disease appears to be spreading among the plants. When this happens, first cease misting, lower the humidity, and give especially good ventilation. Then spray with a general fungicide such as Benlate, Natriphene fungicide (*not* the product called Natriphene S-25), or Anti-Damp. Physan is good for large, tough plants, but can harm small botanicals. Follow directions on the container carefully.

If only one plant is infected, remove it from the area and treat it individually. A diseased spot on a leaf may be dried up and prevented from spreading by smearing on it a paste made from Tersan and a little water, or sometimes by spraying or sponging it with Physan. If this does not halt it, and if other spots appear, the whole leaf may have to be cut off, using a sterile knife. The cut edges may then be smeared with Tersan. To prevent further spread, soak the plant, pot and all, in a solution of Natriphene or Anti-Damp for several hours. Afterward, let the pot dry out and remain dry for a week. As a further precaution, spray with Benlate, which is a systemic fungicide.

Some diseases travel rapidly, and it is not always possible to cure them. Such a disease is a rot that starts either in a leaf or a pseudobulb and moves from there through the plant. It can be halted if caught early. In this case, you may have to cut off a whole growth, leaf and pseudobulb, or even more, watching for clean tissue. Use a freshly sterilized blade for each cut. There may not be much of the plant left, but if it is a valuable one it is worth trying to save. Follow the procedure of soaking and spraying just described.

Monopodials, which have only one growing end, the stem tip, sometimes become infected at this tip. If you see the top leaf becoming infected, remove it at once, and pour Tersan powder into the leaf axil. This usually stops the progress of the disease, but often the stem tip has been killed. The plant will probably make a branch from below this point.

A sheath may turn black and watery, having been attacked by a disease organism. Sponge the sheath or dip the growth in a fungicide, and then cut off the sheath above the enclosed flower buds. Then dip the growth again so that the buds become washed in the fungicide. It may be that the buds have not been affected and can thus be saved. This condition is prevalent where the atmosphere is kept too damp.

In a stagnant, damp atmosphere, flowers may develop pink or brown spots, a blight (*Botrytis*) that spreads quickly if affected flowers are allowed to remain in the presence of other flowers. Cut off all spotted flowers and destroy them. Spray remaining flowers with Natriphene or Anti-Damp, neither of which will harm the blossoms.

Virus diseases are more elusive. They are treacherous because they cannot, at present, be cured, and because they affect the whole plant. All divisions of an infected plant will carry the disease. A virus is spread by cutting a healthy plant with shears or a knife used on a diseased plant, or by insects which transfer juice from one plant to another. Virus diseases may cause streaking of the leaves, fine yellow lines that become dark or black; or a spot that spreads in concentric rings, either round or diamond shape; or pitting on the underside of leaves with the darkened areas showing from the top surface; or "necrotic" areas, areas of dead tissue. One kind shows up in the flowers as a breaking or mottled affect in the color, with sometimes distortion of the flowers. All of these undermine the health of the plant, some to a greater degree than others.

Two viruses known at present, and commonly infecting orchids of almost all genera, are Cymbidium Mosaic Virus (CyMV) and Tobacco Mosaic Virus—Orchid Type (TMV-O). Research is being done on other viruses.

A plant may show such slight symptoms that they go unnoticed. An occasional one may harbor a virus and show no symptoms at all. The same virus that produces drastic damage in one kind of orchid may affect another species only slightly. The reverse is true as well—the virus from a lightly affected plant may do great harm to another. A plant that shows no symptoms itself can act as a "typhoid Mary" and be a source of infection to others. For these various reasons, the precaution of using only sterilized tools is emphasized. When a plant has been proven to have a virus,* or shows unmistakable symptoms, it is wise to dispose of it.

PEST CONTROL

Thrips, spider mites, aphids, scales, and mealy bugs, along with slugs and snails, are the chief enemies of orchids at present. The many pests that attack orchids in their native habitats have been eliminated by modern insecticides here, and have been excluded at the borders by inspection and treatment of imported plants. Those we need to control are therefore kinds that are common to our garden and house plants. Any new plant you acquire should be looked over and if any pests are found it should be cleaned up and treated before being put with the others.

Red spiders and two-spotted mites make minute punctures in the leaves and flowers. Their damage looks like gray stippling on the undersides of leaves, and watery punctures on flowers. They make a fuzzy web on the back of leaves, in which their eggs are laid.

Most ferocious is the false spider mite, a relative of the Cyclamen mite. It is extremely tiny, requiring at least a ten-power lens to be seen, yet it inflicts serious injury. It makes deep brown pits in the leaves, or gray sunken scars. The leaves become distorted and shriveled and fall prematurely. Control for both this and the other spider mites is Kelthane or Chlorobenzilate (or Di-mite if it is available). The former can be bought in an aerosol can. Malathion does not control the false spider mite.

* The Florida West Coast Scientific Laboratories, P. O. Box 11914, Tampa, Florida 33610, tests for virus, for a reasonable fee per sample. Write for information and price per test.

Thrips are small wingless insects that chew the surfaces, particularly of flowers. Aphids need no introduction. Mealy bugs are flat cottony-looking insects, their fluffy appearance produced by a covering of powdery wax. They tend to cluster in protected places such as leaf axils, emerging leaves, and under the covering of rhizomes. There are several kinds of scales; two that are common are a white or grayish hard-shelled one that, like mealy bugs, hides in sheltered places on the plant, and a soft brown scale often found on stems, even flower stems. Malathion and Sevin, used with a spreader-sticker (buy only a kind made for use on plants), will control all of these. Mealy bugs can also be killed by touching each one with a swab dipped in alcohol. However, this gets only those you readily see, and the young crawlers are usually missed. Scales can be scrubbed off with a toothbrush, most easily done during repotting. After such cleaning it is wise to spray with an insecticide for additional control.

Slugs and snails feed on new roots and new growths, flowers and buds, eating fair chunks at a time. There are poisons on the market for these, the effective ingredient of which is metaldehyde. Some come as powders to be sprinkled on the pot surfaces, some as liquids to be watered in. Never use a bait containing arsenic on orchids. Slugs can usually be detected by the slime trail they leave. The little flat-coiled bush snails usually stay within the pot, but can come to the surface to feed on root tips or algae.

The use of poisons in the home must be wisely managed. Where the plants are in a living area extra caution should be used. It would be best to remove the plants to an isolated room, one that can be closed off tightly, before using Malathion or Sevin. There are insecticides put up for house plants that can also be used on orchids. Always hold an aerosol can at some distance from the plants for fear of burning the leaves. Ortho "Indoor Plant Insect Spray" is safe for orchids. Science "Clover Mite and Red

Spider Spray" contains Kelthane and is also safe for orchids. These, too, should be used with caution as advised on the labels, for the protection of human beings as well as that of pets and birds. We do not recommend any systemic insecticide at present.

INDEX

Boldface numbers indicate pages on which illustrations appear.

A CATALOG OF SELECTED
DOVER BOOKS
IN ALL FIELDS OF INTEREST

A CATALOG OF SELECTED DOVER
BOOKS IN ALL FIELDS OF INTEREST

DRAWINGS OF REMBRANDT, edited by Seymour Slive. Updated Lippmann, Hofstede de Groot edition, with definitive scholarly apparatus. All portraits, biblical sketches, landscapes, nudes. Oriental figures, classical studies, together with selection of work by followers. 550 illustrations. Total of 630pp. 9⅛ × 12¼.
21485-0, 21486-9 Pa., Two-vol. set $29.90

GHOST AND HORROR STORIES OF AMBROSE BIERCE, Ambrose Bierce. 24 tales vividly imagined, strangely prophetic, and decades ahead of their time in technical skill: "The Damned Thing," "An Inhabitant of Carcosa," "The Eyes of the Panther," "Moxon's Master," and 20 more. 199pp. 5⅜ × 8½. 20767-6 Pa. $3.95

ETHICAL WRITINGS OF MAIMONIDES, Maimonides. Most significant ethical works of great medieval sage, newly translated for utmost precision, readability. Laws Concerning Character Traits, Eight Chapters, more. 192pp. 5⅜ × 8½.
24522-5 Pa. $4.50

THE EXPLORATION OF THE COLORADO RIVER AND ITS CANYONS, J. W. Powell. Full text of Powell's 1,000-mile expedition down the fabled Colorado in 1869. Superb account of terrain, geology, vegetation, Indians, famine, mutiny, treacherous rapids, mighty canyons, during exploration of last unknown part of continental U.S. 400pp. 5⅜ × 8½. 20094-9 Pa. $7.95

HISTORY OF PHILOSOPHY, Julián Marías. Clearest one-volume history on the market. Every major philosopher and dozens of others, to Existentialism and later. 505pp. 5⅜ × 8½. 21739-6 Pa. $9.95

ALL ABOUT LIGHTNING, Martin A. Uman. Highly readable non-technical survey of nature and causes of lightning, thunderstorms, ball lightning, St. Elmo's Fire, much more. Illustrated. 192pp. 5⅜ × 8½. 25237-X Pa. $5.95

SAILING ALONE AROUND THE WORLD, Captain Joshua Slocum. First man to sail around the world, alone, in small boat. One of great feats of seamanship told in delightful manner. 67 illustrations. 294pp. 5⅜ × 8½. 20326-3 Pa. $4.95

LETTERS AND NOTES ON THE MANNERS, CUSTOMS AND CONDITIONS OF THE NORTH AMERICAN INDIANS, George Catlin. Classic account of life among Plains Indians: ceremonies, hunt, warfare, etc. 312 plates. 572pp. of text. 6⅛ × 9¼. 22118-0, 22119-9, Pa. Two-vol. set $17.90

ALASKA: The Harriman Expedition, 1899, John Burroughs, John Muir, et al. Informative, engrossing accounts of two-month, 9,000-mile expedition. Native peoples, wildlife, forests, geography, salmon industry, glaciers, more. Profusely illustrated. 240 black-and-white line drawings. 124 black-and-white photographs. 3 maps. Index. 576pp. 5⅜ × 8½. 25109-8 Pa. $11.95

THE BOOK OF BEASTS: Being a Translation from a Latin Bestiary of the Twelfth Century, T. H. White. Wonderful catalog real and fanciful beasts: manticore, griffin, phoenix, amphivius, jaculus, many more. White's witty erudite commentary on scientific, historical aspects. Fascinating glimpse of medieval mind. Illustrated. 296pp. 5⅜ × 8¼. (Available in U.S. only) 24609-4 Pa. $6.95

FRANK LLOYD WRIGHT: ARCHITECTURE AND NATURE With 160 Illustrations, Donald Hoffmann. Profusely illustrated study of influence of nature—especially prairie—on Wright's designs for Fallingwater, Robie House, Guggenheim Museum, other masterpieces. 96pp. 9¼ × 10¾. 25098-9 Pa. $7.95

FRANK LLOYD WRIGHT'S FALLINGWATER, Donald Hoffmann. Wright's famous waterfall house: planning and construction of organic idea. History of site, owners, Wright's personal involvement. Photographs of various stages of building. Preface by Edgar Kaufmann, Jr. 100 illustrations. 112pp. 9¼ × 10.
23671-4 Pa. $8.95

YEARS WITH FRANK LLOYD WRIGHT: Apprentice to Genius, Edgar Tafel. Insightful memoir by a former apprentice presents a revealing portrait of Wright the man, the inspired teacher, the greatest American architect. 372 black-and-white illustrations. Preface. Index. vi + 228pp. 8¼ × 11. 24801-1 Pa. $10.95

THE STORY OF KING ARTHUR AND HIS KNIGHTS, Howard Pyle. Enchanting version of King Arthur fable has delighted generations with imaginative narratives of exciting adventures and unforgettable illustrations by the author. 41 illustrations. xviii + 313pp. 6⅛ × 9¼. 21445-1 Pa. $6.95

THE GODS OF THE EGYPTIANS, E. A. Wallis Budge. Thorough coverage of numerous gods of ancient Egypt by foremost Egyptologist. Information on evolution of cults, rites and gods; the cult of Osiris; the Book of the Dead and its rites; the sacred animals and birds; Heaven and Hell; and more. 956pp. 6⅛ × 9¼.
22055-9, 22056-7 Pa., Two-vol. set $21.90

A THEOLOGICO-POLITICAL TREATISE, Benedict Spinoza. Also contains unfinished *Political Treatise*. Great classic on religious liberty, theory of government on common consent. R. Elwes translation. Total of 421pp. 5⅜ × 8½.
20249-6 Pa. $6.95

INCIDENTS OF TRAVEL IN CENTRAL AMERICA, CHIAPAS, AND YUCATAN, John L. Stephens. Almost single-handed discovery of Maya culture; exploration of ruined cities, monuments, temples; customs of Indians. 115 drawings. 892pp. 5⅜ × 8½. 22404-X, 22405-8 Pa., Two-vol. set $15.90

LOS CAPRICHOS, Francisco Goya. 80 plates of wild, grotesque monsters and caricatures. Prado manuscript included. 183pp. 6⅞ × 9⅜. 22384-1 Pa. $5.95

AUTOBIOGRAPHY: The Story of My Experiments with Truth, Mohandas K. Gandhi. Not hagiography, but Gandhi in his own words. Boyhood, legal studies, purification, the growth of the Satyagraha (nonviolent protest) movement. Critical, inspiring work of the man who freed India. 480pp. 5⅜ × 8½. (Available in U.S. only)
24593-4 Pa. $6.95

ILLUSTRATED DICTIONARY OF HISTORIC ARCHITECTURE, edited by Cyril M. Harris. Extraordinary compendium of clear, concise definitions for over 5,000 important architectural terms complemented by over 2,000 line drawings. Covers full spectrum of architecture from ancient ruins to 20th-century Modernism. Preface. 592pp. 7½ × 9⅜. 24444-X Pa. $15.95

THE NIGHT BEFORE CHRISTMAS, Clement Moore. Full text, and woodcuts from original 1848 book. Also critical, historical material. 19 illustrations. 40pp. 4⅝ × 6. 22797-9 Pa. $2.50

THE LESSON OF JAPANESE ARCHITECTURE: 165 Photographs, Jiro Harada. Memorable gallery of 165 photographs taken in the 1930's of exquisite Japanese homes of the well-to-do and historic buildings. 13 line diagrams. 192pp. 8⅜ × 11¼. 24778-3 Pa. $10.95

THE AUTOBIOGRAPHY OF CHARLES DARWIN AND SELECTED LETTERS, edited by Francis Darwin. The fascinating life of eccentric genius composed of an intimate memoir by Darwin (intended for his children); commentary by his son, Francis; hundreds of fragments from notebooks, journals, papers; and letters to and from Lyell, Hooker, Huxley, Wallace and Henslow. xi + 365pp. 5⅜ × 8. 20479-0 Pa. $6.95

WONDERS OF THE SKY: Observing Rainbows, Comets, Eclipses, the Stars and Other Phenomena, Fred Schaaf. Charming, easy-to-read poetic guide to all manner of celestial events visible to the naked eye. Mock suns, glories, Belt of Venus, more. Illustrated. 299pp. 5¼ × 8¼. 24402-4 Pa. $7.95

BURNHAM'S CELESTIAL HANDBOOK, Robert Burnham, Jr. Thorough guide to the stars beyond our solar system. Exhaustive treatment. Alphabetical by constellation: Andromeda to Cetus in Vol. 1; Chamaeleon to Orion in Vol. 2; and Pavo to Vulpecula in Vol. 3. Hundreds of illustrations. Index in Vol. 3. 2,000pp. 6⅛ × 9¼. 23567-X, 23568-8, 23673-0 Pa., Three-vol. set $38.85

STAR NAMES: Their Lore and Meaning, Richard Hinckley Allen. Fascinating history of names various cultures have given to constellations and literary and folkloristic uses that have been made of stars. Indexes to subjects. Arabic and Greek names. Biblical references. Bibliography. 563pp. 5⅜ × 8½. 21079-0 Pa. $8.95

THIRTY YEARS THAT SHOOK PHYSICS: The Story of Quantum Theory, George Gamow. Lucid, accessible introduction to influential theory of energy and matter. Careful explanations of Dirac's anti-particles, Bohr's model of the atom, much more. 12 plates. Numerous drawings. 240pp. 5⅜ × 8½. 24895-X Pa. $5.95

CHINESE DOMESTIC FURNITURE IN PHOTOGRAPHS AND MEASURED DRAWINGS, Gustav Ecke. A rare volume, now affordably priced for antique collectors, furniture buffs and art historians. Detailed review of styles ranging from early Shang to late Ming. Unabridged republication. 161 black-and-white drawings, photos. Total of 224pp. 8⅜ × 11¼. (Available in U.S. only) 25171-3 Pa. $13.95

VINCENT VAN GOGH: A Biography, Julius Meier-Graefe. Dynamic, penetrating study of artist's life, relationship with brother, Theo, painting techniques, travels, more. Readable, engrossing. 160pp. 5⅜ × 8½. (Available in U.S. only) 25253-1 Pa. $4.95

HOW TO WRITE, Gertrude Stein. Gertrude Stein claimed anyone could understand her unconventional writing—here are clues to help. Fascinating improvisations, language experiments, explanations illuminate Stein's craft and the art of writing. Total of 414pp. 4⅝ × 6⅜. 23144-5 Pa. $6.95

ADVENTURES AT SEA IN THE GREAT AGE OF SAIL: Five Firsthand Narratives, edited by Elliot Snow. Rare true accounts of exploration, whaling, shipwreck, fierce natives, trade, shipboard life, more. 33 illustrations. Introduction. 353pp. 5⅜ × 8½. 25177-2 Pa. $8.95

THE HERBAL OR GENERAL HISTORY OF PLANTS, John Gerard. Classic descriptions of about 2,850 plants—with over 2,700 illustrations—includes Latin and English names, physical descriptions, varieties, time and place of growth, more. 2,706 illustrations. xlv + 1,678pp. 8½ × 12¼. 23147-X Cloth. $75.00

DOROTHY AND THE WIZARD IN OZ, L. Frank Baum. Dorothy and the Wizard visit the center of the Earth, where people are vegetables, glass houses grow and Oz characters reappear. Classic sequel to *Wizard of Oz*. 256pp. 5⅜ × 8.

24714-7 Pa. $4.95

SONGS OF EXPERIENCE: Facsimile Reproduction with 26 Plates in Full Color, William Blake. This facsimile of Blake's original "Illuminated Book" reproduces 26 full-color plates from a rare 1826 edition. Includes "The Tyger," "London," "Holy Thursday," and other immortal poems. 26 color plates. Printed text of poems. 48pp. 5¼ × 7. 24636-1 Pa. $3.50

SONGS OF INNOCENCE, William Blake. The first and most popular of Blake's famous "Illuminated Books," in a facsimile edition reproducing all 31 brightly colored plates. Additional printed text of each poem. 64pp. 5¼ × 7.

22764-2 Pa. $3.50

PRECIOUS STONES, Max Bauer. Classic, thorough study of diamonds, rubies, emeralds, garnets, etc.: physical character, occurrence, properties, use, similar topics. 20 plates, 8 in color. 94 figures. 659pp. 6⅛ × 9¼.

21910-0, 21911-9 Pa., Two-vol. set $15.90

ENCYCLOPEDIA OF VICTORIAN NEEDLEWORK, S. F. A. Caulfeild and Blanche Saward. Full, precise descriptions of stitches, techniques for dozens of needlecrafts—most exhaustive reference of its kind. Over 800 figures. Total of 679pp. 8⅛ × 11. Two volumes. Vol. 1 22800-2 Pa. $11.95
Vol. 2 22801-0 Pa. $11.95

THE MARVELOUS LAND OF OZ, L. Frank Baum. Second Oz book, the Scarecrow and Tin Woodman are back with hero named Tip, Oz magic. 136 illustrations. 287pp. 5⅜ × 8½. 20692-0 Pa. $5.95

WILD FOWL DECOYS, Joel Barber. Basic book on the subject, by foremost authority and collector. Reveals history of decoy making and rigging, place in American culture, different kinds of decoys, how to make them, and how to use them. 140 plates. 156pp. 7⅞ × 10¾. 20011-6 Pa. $8.95

HISTORY OF LACE, Mrs. Bury Palliser. Definitive, profusely illustrated chronicle of lace from earliest times to late 19th century. Laces of Italy, Greece, England, France, Belgium, etc. Landmark of needlework scholarship. 266 illustrations. 672pp. 6⅛ × 9¼. 24742-2 Pa. $14.95

ILLUSTRATED GUIDE TO SHAKER FURNITURE, Robert Meader. All furniture and appurtenances, with much on unknown local styles. 235 photos. 146pp. 9 × 12. 22819-3 Pa. $8.95

WHALE SHIPS AND WHALING: A Pictorial Survey, George Francis Dow. Over 200 vintage engravings, drawings, photographs of barks, brigs, cutters, other vessels. Also harpoons, lances, whaling guns, many other artifacts. Comprehensive text by foremost authority. 207 black-and-white illustrations. 288pp. 6 × 9. 24808-9 Pa. $8.95

THE BERTRAMS, Anthony Trollope. Powerful portrayal of blind self-will and thwarted ambition includes one of Trollope's most heartrending love stories. 497pp. 5⅜ × 8½. 25119-5 Pa. $9.95

ADVENTURES WITH A HAND LENS, Richard Headstrom. Clearly written guide to observing and studying flowers and grasses, fish scales, moth and insect wings, egg cases, buds, feathers, seeds, leaf scars, moss, molds, ferns, common crystals, etc.—all with an ordinary, inexpensive magnifying glass. 209 exact line drawings aid in your discoveries. 220pp. 5⅜ × 8½. 23330-8 Pa. $4.95

RODIN ON ART AND ARTISTS, Auguste Rodin. Great sculptor's candid, wide-ranging comments on meaning of art; great artists; relation of sculpture to poetry, painting, music; philosophy of life, more. 76 superb black-and-white illustrations of Rodin's sculpture, drawings and prints. 119pp. 8⅜ × 11¼. 24487-3 Pa. $7.95

FIFTY CLASSIC FRENCH FILMS, 1912–1982: A Pictorial Record, Anthony Slide. Memorable stills from Grand Illusion, Beauty and the Beast, Hiroshima, Mon Amour, many more. Credits, plot synopses, reviews, etc. 160pp. 8¼ × 11. 25256-6 Pa. $11.95

THE PRINCIPLES OF PSYCHOLOGY, William James. Famous long course complete, unabridged. Stream of thought, time perception, memory, experimental methods; great work decades ahead of its time. 94 figures. 1,391pp. 5⅜ × 8½. 20381-6, 20382-4 Pa., Two-vol. set $23.90

BODIES IN A BOOKSHOP, R. T. Campbell. Challenging mystery of blackmail and murder with ingenious plot and superbly drawn characters. In the best tradition of British suspense fiction. 192pp. 5⅜ × 8½. 24720-1 Pa. $3.95

CALLAS: PORTRAIT OF A PRIMA DONNA, George Jellinek. Renowned commentator on the musical scene chronicles incredible career and life of the most controversial, fascinating, influential operatic personality of our time. 64 black-and-white photographs. 416pp. 5⅜ × 8¼. 25047-4 Pa. $8.95

GEOMETRY, RELATIVITY AND THE FOURTH DIMENSION, Rudolph Rucker. Exposition of fourth dimension, concepts of relativity as Flatland characters continue adventures. Popular, easily followed yet accurate, profound. 141 illustrations. 133pp. 5⅜ × 8½. 23400-2 Pa. $3.95

HOUSEHOLD STORIES BY THE BROTHERS GRIMM, with pictures by Walter Crane. 53 classic stories—Rumpelstiltskin, Rapunzel, Hansel and Gretel, the Fisherman and his Wife, Snow White, Tom Thumb, Sleeping Beauty, Cinderella, and so much more—lavishly illustrated with original 19th century drawings. 114 illustrations. x + 269pp. 5⅜ × 8½. 21080-4 Pa. $4.95

SUNDIALS, Albert Waugh. Far and away the best, most thorough coverage of ideas, mathematics concerned, types, construction, adjusting anywhere. Over 100 illustrations. 230pp. 5⅜ × 8½. 22947-5 Pa. $4.95

PICTURE HISTORY OF THE NORMANDIE: With 190 Illustrations, Frank O. Braynard. Full story of legendary French ocean liner: Art Deco interiors, design innovations, furnishings, celebrities, maiden voyage, tragic fire, much more. Extensive text. 144pp. 8⅞ × 11¾. 25257-4 Pa. $10.95

THE FIRST AMERICAN COOKBOOK: A Facsimile of "American Cookery," 1796, Amelia Simmons. Facsimile of the first American-written cookbook published in the United States contains authentic recipes for colonial favorites—pumpkin pudding, winter squash pudding, spruce beer, Indian slapjacks, and more. Introductory Essay and Glossary of colonial cooking terms. 80pp. 5⅜ × 8½. 24710-4 Pa. $3.50

101 PUZZLES IN THOUGHT AND LOGIC, C. R. Wylie, Jr. Solve murders and robberies, find out which fishermen are liars, how a blind man could possibly identify a color—purely by your own reasoning! 107pp. 5⅜ × 8½. 20367-0 Pa. $2.50

THE BOOK OF WORLD-FAMOUS MUSIC—CLASSICAL, POPULAR AND FOLK, James J. Fuld. Revised and enlarged republication of landmark work in musico-bibliography. Full information about nearly 1,000 songs and compositions including first lines of music and lyrics. New supplement. Index. 800pp. 5⅜ × 8¼. 24857-7 Pa. $15.95

ANTHROPOLOGY AND MODERN LIFE, Franz Boas. Great anthropologist's classic treatise on race and culture. Introduction by Ruth Bunzel. Only inexpensive paperback edition. 255pp. 5⅜ × 8½. 25245-0 Pa. $6.95

THE TALE OF PETER RABBIT, Beatrix Potter. The inimitable Peter's terrifying adventure in Mr. McGregor's garden, with all 27 wonderful, full-color Potter illustrations. 55pp. 4¼ × 5½. (Available in U.S. only) 22827-4 Pa. $1.75

THREE PROPHETIC SCIENCE FICTION NOVELS, H. G. Wells. *When the Sleeper Wakes, A Story of the Days to Come* and *The Time Machine* (full version). 335pp. 5⅜ × 8½. (Available in U.S. only) 20605-X Pa. $6.95

APICIUS COOKERY AND DINING IN IMPERIAL ROME, edited and translated by Joseph Dommers Vehling. Oldest known cookbook in existence offers readers a clear picture of what foods Romans ate, how they prepared them, etc. 49 illustrations. 301pp. 6⅛ × 9¼. 23563-7 Pa. $7.95

SHAKESPEARE LEXICON AND QUOTATION DICTIONARY, Alexander Schmidt. Full definitions, locations, shades of meaning of every word in plays and poems. More than 50,000 exact quotations. 1,485pp. 6½ × 9¼. 22726-X, 22727-8 Pa., Two-vol. set $29.90

THE WORLD'S GREAT SPEECHES, edited by Lewis Copeland and Lawrence W. Lamm. Vast collection of 278 speeches from Greeks to 1970. Powerful and effective models; unique look at history. 842pp. 5⅜ × 8½. 20468-5 Pa. $11.95

CATALOG OF DOVER BOOKS

THE BLUE FAIRY BOOK, Andrew Lang. The first, most famous collection, with many familiar tales: Little Red Riding Hood, Aladdin and the Wonderful Lamp, Puss in Boots, Sleeping Beauty, Hansel and Gretel, Rumpelstiltskin; 37 in all. 138 illustrations. 390pp. 5⅜ × 8½.   21437-0 Pa. $6.95

THE STORY OF THE CHAMPIONS OF THE ROUND TABLE, Howard Pyle. Sir Launcelot, Sir Tristram and Sir Percival in spirited adventures of love and triumph retold in Pyle's inimitable style. 50 drawings, 31 full-page. xviii + 329pp. 6½ × 9¼.   21883-X Pa. $7.95

AUDUBON AND HIS JOURNALS, Maria Audubon. Unmatched two-volume portrait of the great artist, naturalist and author contains his journals, an excellent biography by his granddaughter, expert annotations by the noted ornithologist, Dr. Elliott Coues, and 37 superb illustrations. Total of 1,200pp. 5⅜ × 8.

Vol. I 25143-8 Pa. $8.95
Vol. II 25144-6 Pa. $8.95

GREAT DINOSAUR HUNTERS AND THEIR DISCOVERIES, Edwin H. Colbert. Fascinating, lavishly illustrated chronicle of dinosaur research, 1820's to 1960. Achievements of Cope, Marsh, Brown, Buckland, Mantell, Huxley, many others. 384pp. 5¼ × 8¼.   24701-5 Pa. $7.95

THE TASTEMAKERS, Russell Lynes. Informal, illustrated social history of American taste 1850's–1950's. First popularized categories Highbrow, Lowbrow, Middlebrow. 129 illustrations. New (1979) afterword. 384pp. 6 × 9.

23993-4 Pa. $8.95

DOUBLE CROSS PURPOSES, Ronald A. Knox. A treasure hunt in the Scottish Highlands, an old map, unidentified corpse, surprise discoveries keep reader guessing in this cleverly intricate tale of financial skullduggery. 2 black-and-white maps. 320pp. 5⅜ × 8½. (Available in U.S. only)   25032-6 Pa. $6.95

AUTHENTIC VICTORIAN DECORATION AND ORNAMENTATION IN FULL COLOR: 46 Plates from "Studies in Design," Christopher Dresser. Superb full-color lithographs reproduced from rare original portfolio of a major Victorian designer. 48pp. 9¼ × 12¼.   25083-0 Pa. $7.95

PRIMITIVE ART, Franz Boas. Remains the best text ever prepared on subject, thoroughly discussing Indian, African, Asian, Australian, and, especially, North-ern American primitive art. Over 950 illustrations show ceramics, masks, totem poles, weapons, textiles, paintings, much more. 376pp. 5⅜ × 8.   20025-6 Pa. $6.95

SIDELIGHTS ON RELATIVITY, Albert Einstein. Unabridged republication of two lectures delivered by the great physicist in 1920–21. *Ether and Relativity* and *Geometry and Experience.* Elegant ideas in non-mathematical form, accessible to intelligent layman. vi + 56pp. 5⅜ × 8½.   24511-X Pa. $2.95

THE WIT AND HUMOR OF OSCAR WILDE, edited by Alvin Redman. More than 1,000 ripostes, paradoxes, wisecracks: Work is the curse of the drinking classes, I can resist everything except temptation, etc. 258pp. 5⅜ × 8½.   20602-5 Pa. $4.95

ADVENTURES WITH A MICROSCOPE, Richard Headstrom. 59 adventures with clothing fibers, protozoa, ferns and lichens, roots and leaves, much more. 142 illustrations. 232pp. 5⅜ × 8½.   23471-1 Pa. $3.95

PLANTS OF THE BIBLE, Harold N. Moldenke and Alma L. Moldenke. Standard reference to all 230 plants mentioned in Scriptures. Latin name, biblical reference, uses, modern identity, much more. Unsurpassed encyclopedic resource for scholars, botanists, nature lovers, students of Bible. Bibliography. Indexes. 123 black-and-white illustrations. 384pp. 6 × 9. 25069-5 Pa. $8.95

FAMOUS AMERICAN WOMEN: A Biographical Dictionary from Colonial Times to the Present, Robert McHenry, ed. From Pocahontas to Rosa Parks, 1,035 distinguished American women documented in separate biographical entries. Accurate, up-to-date data, numerous categories, spans 400 years. Indices. 493pp. 6½ × 9¼. 24523-3 Pa. $10.95

THE FABULOUS INTERIORS OF THE GREAT OCEAN LINERS IN HISTORIC PHOTOGRAPHS, William H. Miller, Jr. Some 200 superb photographs capture exquisite interiors of world's great "floating palaces"—1890's to 1980's: *Titanic, Ile de France, Queen Elizabeth, United States, Europa,* more. Approx. 200 black-and-white photographs. Captions. Text. Introduction. 160pp. 8⅞ × 11¾. 24756-2 Pa. $9.95

THE GREAT LUXURY LINERS, 1927–1954: A Photographic Record, William H. Miller, Jr. Nostalgic tribute to heyday of ocean liners. 186 photos of Ile de France, Normandie, Leviathan, Queen Elizabeth, United States, many others. Interior and exterior views. Introduction. Captions. 160pp. 9 × 12. 24056-8 Pa. $10.95

A NATURAL HISTORY OF THE DUCKS, John Charles Phillips. Great landmark of ornithology offers complete detailed coverage of nearly 200 species and subspecies of ducks: gadwall, sheldrake, merganser, pintail, many more. 74 full-color plates, 102 black-and-white. Bibliography. Total of 1,920pp. 8⅝ × 11¼. 25141-1, 25142-X Cloth. Two-vol. set $100.00

THE SEAWEED HANDBOOK: An Illustrated Guide to Seaweeds from North Carolina to Canada, Thomas F. Lee. Concise reference covers 78 species. Scientific and common names, habitat, distribution, more. Finding keys for easy identification. 224pp. 5⅜ × 8½. 25215-9 Pa. $6.95

THE TEN BOOKS OF ARCHITECTURE: The 1755 Leoni Edition, Leon Battista Alberti. Rare classic helped introduce the glories of ancient architecture to the Renaissance. 68 black-and-white plates. 336pp. 8⅜ × 11¼. 25239-6 Pa. $14.95

MISS MACKENZIE, Anthony Trollope. Minor masterpieces by Victorian master unmasks many truths about life in 19th-century England. First inexpensive edition in years. 392pp. 5⅜ × 8½. 25201-9 Pa. $8.95

THE RIME OF THE ANCIENT MARINER, Gustave Doré, Samuel Taylor Coleridge. Dramatic engravings considered by many to be his greatest work. The terrifying space of the open sea, the storms and whirlpools of an unknown ocean, the ice of Antarctica, more—all rendered in a powerful, chilling manner. Full text. 38 plates. 77pp. 9¼ × 12. 22305-1 Pa. $4.95

THE EXPEDITIONS OF ZEBULON MONTGOMERY PIKE, Zebulon Montgomery Pike. Fascinating first-hand accounts (1805–6) of exploration of Mississippi River, Indian wars, capture by Spanish dragoons, much more. 1,088pp. 5⅜ × 8½. 25254-X, 25255-8 Pa. Two-vol. set $25.90

A CONCISE HISTORY OF PHOTOGRAPHY: Third Revised Edition, Helmut Gernsheim. Best one-volume history—camera obscura, photochemistry, daguerreotypes, evolution of cameras, film, more. Also artistic aspects—landscape, portraits, fine art, etc. 281 black-and-white photographs. 26 in color. 176pp. 8⅜ × 11¼. 25128-4 Pa. $13.95

THE DORÉ BIBLE ILLUSTRATIONS, Gustave Doré. 241 detailed plates from the Bible: the Creation scenes, Adam and Eve, Flood, Babylon, battle sequences, life of Jesus, etc. Each plate is accompanied by the verses from the King James version of the Bible. 241pp. 9 × 12. 23004-X Pa. $9.95

HUGGER-MUGGER IN THE LOUVRE, Elliot Paul. Second Homer Evans mystery-comedy. Theft at the Louvre involves sleuth in hilarious, madcap caper. "A knockout."—Books. 336pp. 5⅜ × 8½. 25185-3 Pa. $5.95

FLATLAND, E. A. Abbott. Intriguing and enormously popular science-fiction classic explores the complexities of trying to survive as a two-dimensional being in a three-dimensional world. Amusingly illustrated by the author. 16 illustrations. 103pp. 5⅜ × 8½. 20001-9 Pa. $2.50

THE HISTORY OF THE LEWIS AND CLARK EXPEDITION, Meriwether Lewis and William Clark, edited by Elliott Coues. Classic edition of Lewis and Clark's day-by-day journals that later became the basis for U.S. claims to Oregon and the West. Accurate and invaluable geographical, botanical, biological, meteorological and anthropological material. Total of 1,508pp. 5⅜ × 8½.
21268-8, 21269-6, 21270-X Pa. Three-vol. set $26.85

LANGUAGE, TRUTH AND LOGIC, Alfred J. Ayer. Famous, clear introduction to Vienna, Cambridge schools of Logical Positivism. Role of philosophy, elimination of metaphysics, nature of analysis, etc. 160pp. 5⅜ × 8½. (Available in U.S. and Canada only) 20010-8 Pa. $3.95

MATHEMATICS FOR THE NONMATHEMATICIAN, Morris Kline. Detailed, college-level treatment of mathematics in cultural and historical context, with numerous exercises. For liberal arts students. Preface. Recommended Reading Lists. Tables. Index. Numerous black-and-white figures. xvi + 641pp. 5⅜ × 8½.
24823-2 Pa. $11.95

HANDBOOK OF PICTORIAL SYMBOLS, Rudolph Modley. 3,250 signs and symbols, many systems in full; official or heavy commercial use. Arranged by subject. Most in Pictorial Archive series. 143pp. 8⅛ × 11. 23357-X Pa. $6.95

INCIDENTS OF TRAVEL IN YUCATAN, John L. Stephens. Classic (1843) exploration of jungles of Yucatan, looking for evidences of Maya civilization. Travel adventures, Mexican and Indian culture, etc. Total of 669pp. 5⅜ × 8½.
20926-1, 20927-X Pa., Two-vol. set $11.90

DEGAS: An Intimate Portrait, Ambroise Vollard. Charming, anecdotal memoir by famous art dealer of one of the greatest 19th-century French painters. 14 black-and-white illustrations. Introduction by Harold L. Van Doren. 96pp. 5⅜ × 8½.
25131-4 Pa. $4.95

PERSONAL NARRATIVE OF A PILGRIMAGE TO ALMANDINAH AND MECCAH, Richard Burton. Great travel classic by remarkably colorful personality. Burton, disguised as a Moroccan, visited sacred shrines of Islam, narrowly escaping death. 47 illustrations. 959pp. 5⅜ × 8½. 21217-3, 21218-1 Pa., Two-vol. set $19.90

PHRASE AND WORD ORIGINS, A. H. Holt. Entertaining, reliable, modern study of more than 1,200 colorful words, phrases, origins and histories. Much unexpected information. 254pp. 5⅜ × 8½. 20758-7 Pa. $5.95

THE RED THUMB MARK, R. Austin Freeman. In this first Dr. Thorndyke case, the great scientific detective draws fascinating conclusions from the nature of a single fingerprint. Exciting story, authentic science. 320pp. 5⅜ × 8½. (Available in U.S. only) 25210-8 Pa. $6.95

AN EGYPTIAN HIEROGLYPHIC DICTIONARY, E. A. Wallis Budge. Monumental work containing about 25,000 words or terms that occur in texts ranging from 3000 B.C. to 600 A.D. Each entry consists of a transliteration of the word, the word in hieroglyphs, and the meaning in English. 1,314pp. 6⅝ × 10.
23615-3, 23616-1 Pa., Two-vol. set $31.90

THE COMPLEAT STRATEGYST: Being a Primer on the Theory of Games of Strategy, J. D. Williams. Highly entertaining classic describes, with many illustrated examples, how to select best strategies in conflict situations. Prefaces. Appendices. xvi + 268pp. 5⅜ × 8½. 25101-2 Pa. $5.95

THE ROAD TO OZ, L. Frank Baum. Dorothy meets the Shaggy Man, little Button-Bright and the Rainbow's beautiful daughter in this delightful trip to the magical Land of Oz. 272pp. 5⅜ × 8. 25208-6 Pa. $5.95

POINT AND LINE TO PLANE, Wassily Kandinsky. Seminal exposition of role of point, line, other elements in non-objective painting. Essential to understanding 20th-century art. 127 illustrations. 192pp. 6½ × 9¼. 23808-3 Pa. $4.95

LADY ANNA, Anthony Trollope. Moving chronicle of Countess Lovel's bitter struggle to win for herself and daughter Anna their rightful rank and fortune—perhaps at cost of sanity itself. 384pp. 5⅜ × 8½. 24669-8 Pa. $8.95

EGYPTIAN MAGIC, E. A. Wallis Budge. Sums up all that is known about magic in Ancient Egypt: the role of magic in controlling the gods, powerful amulets that warded off evil spirits, scarabs of immortality, use of wax images, formulas and spells, the secret name, much more. 253pp. 5⅜ × 8½. 22681-6 Pa. $4.50

THE DANCE OF SIVA, Ananda Coomaraswamy. Preeminent authority unfolds the vast metaphysic of India: the revelation of her art, conception of the universe, social organization, etc. 27 reproductions of art masterpieces. 192pp. 5⅜ × 8½.
24817-8 Pa. $5.95

CATALOG OF DOVER BOOKS

CHRISTMAS CUSTOMS AND TRADITIONS, Clement A. Miles. Origin, evolution, significance of religious, secular practices. Caroling, gifts, yule logs, much more. Full, scholarly yet fascinating; non-sectarian. 400pp. 5⅜ × 8½.
23354-5 Pa. $6.95

THE HUMAN FIGURE IN MOTION, Eadweard Muybridge. More than 4,500 stopped-action photos, in action series, showing undraped men, women, children jumping, lying down, throwing, sitting, wrestling, carrying, etc. 390pp. 7⅞ × 10⅝.
20204-6 Cloth. $21.95

THE MAN WHO WAS THURSDAY, Gilbert Keith Chesterton. Witty, fast-paced novel about a club of anarchists in turn-of-the-century London. Brilliant social, religious, philosophical speculations. 128pp. 5⅜ × 8½.
25121-7 Pa. $3.95

A CEZANNE SKETCHBOOK: Figures, Portraits, Landscapes and Still Lifes, Paul Cezanne. Great artist experiments with tonal effects, light, mass, other qualities in over 100 drawings. A revealing view of developing master painter, precursor of Cubism. 102 black-and-white illustrations. 144pp. 8¾ × 6⅜.
24790-2 Pa. $5.95

AN ENCYCLOPEDIA OF BATTLES: Accounts of Over 1,560 Battles from 1479 B.C. to the Present, David Eggenberger. Presents essential details of every major battle in recorded history, from the first battle of Megiddo in 1479 B.C. to Grenada in 1984. List of Battle Maps. New Appendix covering the years 1967–1984. Index. 99 illustrations. 544pp. 6½ × 9¼.
24913-1 Pa. $14.95

AN ETYMOLOGICAL DICTIONARY OF MODERN ENGLISH, Ernest Weekley. Richest, fullest work, by foremost British lexicographer. Detailed word histories. Inexhaustible. Total of 856pp. 6½ × 9¼.
21873-2, 21874-0 Pa., Two-vol. set $17.00

WEBSTER'S AMERICAN MILITARY BIOGRAPHIES, edited by Robert McHenry. Over 1,000 figures who shaped 3 centuries of American military history. Detailed biographies of Nathan Hale, Douglas MacArthur, Mary Hallaren, others. Chronologies of engagements, more. Introduction. Addenda. 1,033 entries in alphabetical order. xi + 548pp. 6½ × 9¼. (Available in U.S. only)
24758-9 Pa. $13.95

LIFE IN ANCIENT EGYPT, Adolf Erman. Detailed older account, with much not in more recent books: domestic life, religion, magic, medicine, commerce, and whatever else needed for complete picture. Many illustrations. 597pp. 5⅜ × 8½.
22632-8 Pa. $8.95

HISTORIC COSTUME IN PICTURES, Braun & Schneider. Over 1,450 costumed figures shown, covering a wide variety of peoples: kings, emperors, nobles, priests, servants, soldiers, scholars, townsfolk, peasants, merchants, courtiers, cavaliers, and more. 256pp. 8⅜ × 11¼.
23150-X Pa. $9.95

THE NOTEBOOKS OF LEONARDO DA VINCI, edited by J. P. Richter. Extracts from manuscripts reveal great genius; on painting, sculpture, anatomy, sciences, geography, etc. Both Italian and English. 186 ms. pages reproduced, plus 500 additional drawings, including studies for *Last Supper, Sforza* monument, etc. 860pp. 7⅞ × 10¾. (Available in U.S. only) 22572-0, 22573-9 Pa., Two-vol. set $31.90

THE ART NOUVEAU STYLE BOOK OF ALPHONSE MUCHA: All 72 Plates from "Documents Decoratifs" in Original Color, Alphonse Mucha. Rare copyright-free design portfolio by high priest of Art Nouveau. Jewelry, wallpaper, stained glass, furniture, figure studies, plant and animal motifs, etc. Only complete one-volume edition. 80pp. 9⅜ × 12¼. 24044-4 Pa. $9.95

ANIMALS: 1,419 COPYRIGHT-FREE ILLUSTRATIONS OF MAMMALS, BIRDS, FISH, INSECTS, ETC., edited by Jim Harter. Clear wood engravings present, in extremely lifelike poses, over 1,000 species of animals. One of the most extensive pictorial sourcebooks of its kind. Captions. Index. 284pp. 9 × 12.
23766-4 Pa. $9.95

OBELISTS FLY HIGH, C. Daly King. Masterpiece of American detective fiction, long out of print, involves murder on a 1935 transcontinental flight—"a very thrilling story"—NY Times. Unabridged and unaltered republication of the edition published by William Collins Sons & Co. Ltd., London, 1935. 288pp. 5⅜ × 8½. (Available in U.S. only) 25036-9 Pa. $5.95

VICTORIAN AND EDWARDIAN FASHION: A Photographic Survey, Alison Gernsheim. First fashion history completely illustrated by contemporary photographs. Full text plus 235 photos, 1840–1914, in which many celebrities appear. 240pp. 6½ × 9¼. 24205-6 Pa. $6.95

THE ART OF THE FRENCH ILLUSTRATED BOOK, 1700–1914, Gordon N. Ray. Over 630 superb book illustrations by Fragonard, Delacroix, Daumier, Doré, Grandville, Manet, Mucha, Steinlen, Toulouse-Lautrec and many others. Preface. Introduction. 633 halftones. Indices of artists, authors & titles, binders and provenances. Appendices. Bibliography. 608pp. 8⅜ × 11¼. 25086-5 Pa. $24.95

THE WONDERFUL WIZARD OF OZ, L. Frank Baum. Facsimile in full color of America's finest children's classic. 143 illustrations by W. W. Denslow. 267pp. 5⅜ × 8½. 20691-2 Pa. $7.95

FRONTIERS OF MODERN PHYSICS: New Perspectives on Cosmology, Relativity, Black Holes and Extraterrestrial Intelligence, Tony Rothman, et al. For the intelligent layman. Subjects include: cosmological models of the universe; black holes; the neutrino; the search for extraterrestrial intelligence. Introduction. 46 black-and-white illustrations. 192pp. 5⅜ × 8½. 24587-X Pa. $7.95

THE FRIENDLY STARS, Martha Evans Martin & Donald Howard Menzel. Classic text marshalls the stars together in an engaging, non-technical survey, presenting them as sources of beauty in night sky. 23 illustrations. Foreword. 2 star charts. Index. 147pp. 5⅜ × 8½. 21099-5 Pa. $3.95

FADS AND FALLACIES IN THE NAME OF SCIENCE, Martin Gardner. Fair, witty appraisal of cranks, quacks, and quackeries of science and pseudoscience: hollow earth, Velikovsky, orgone energy, Dianetics, flying saucers, Bridey Murphy, food and medical fads, etc. Revised, expanded In the Name of Science. "A very able and even-tempered presentation."—The New Yorker. 363pp. 5⅜ × 8.
20394-8 Pa. $6.95

ANCIENT EGYPT: ITS CULTURE AND HISTORY, J. E Manchip White. From pre-dynastics through Ptolemies: society, history, political structure, religion, daily life, literature, cultural heritage. 48 plates. 217pp. 5⅜ × 8½. 22548-8 Pa. $5.95

SIR HARRY HOTSPUR OF HUMBLETHWAITE, Anthony Trollope. Incisive, unconventional psychological study of a conflict between a wealthy baronet, his idealistic daughter, and their scapegrace cousin. The 1870 novel in its first inexpensive edition in years. 250pp. 5⅜ × 8½. 24953-0 Pa. $5.95

LASERS AND HOLOGRAPHY, Winston E. Kock. Sound introduction to burgeoning field, expanded (1981) for second edition. Wave patterns, coherence, lasers, diffraction, zone plates, properties of holograms, recent advances. 84 illustrations. 160pp. 5⅜ × 8¼. (Except in United Kingdom) 24041-X Pa. $3.95

INTRODUCTION TO ARTIFICIAL INTELLIGENCE: SECOND, EN-LARGED EDITION, Philip C. Jackson, Jr. Comprehensive survey of artificial intelligence—the study of how machines (computers) can be made to act intelligently. Includes introductory and advanced material. Extensive notes updating the main text. 132 black-and-white illustrations. 512pp. 5⅜ × 8½. 24864-X Pa. $8.95

HISTORY OF INDIAN AND INDONESIAN ART, Ananda K. Coomaraswamy. Over 400 illustrations illuminate classic study of Indian art from earliest Harappa finds to early 20th century. Provides philosophical, religious and social insights. 304pp. 6⅝ × 9⅜. 25005-9 Pa. $9.95

THE GOLEM, Gustav Meyrink. Most famous supernatural novel in modern European literature, set in Ghetto of Old Prague around 1890. Compelling story of mystical experiences, strange transformations, profound terror. 13 black-and-white illustrations. 224pp. 5⅜ × 8½. (Available in U.S. only) 25025-3 Pa. $6.95

ARMADALE, Wilkie Collins. Third great mystery novel by the author of *The Woman in White* and *The Moonstone*. Original magazine version with 40 illustrations. 597pp. 5⅜ × 8½. 23429-0 Pa. $9.95

PICTORIAL ENCYCLOPEDIA OF HISTORIC ARCHITECTURAL PLANS, DETAILS AND ELEMENTS: With 1,880 Line Drawings of Arches, Domes, Doorways, Facades, Gables, Windows, etc., John Theodore Haneman. Sourcebook of inspiration for architects, designers, others. Bibliography. Captions. 141pp. 9 × 12. 24605-1 Pa. $7.95

BENCHLEY LOST AND FOUND, Robert Benchley. Finest humor from early 30's, about pet peeves, child psychologists, post office and others. Mostly unavailable elsewhere. 73 illustrations by Peter Arno and others. 183pp. 5⅜ × 8½.
22410-4 Pa. $4.95

ERTÉ GRAPHICS, Erté. Collection of striking color graphics: *Seasons, Alphabet, Numerals, Aces* and *Precious Stones*. 50 plates, including 4 on covers. 48pp. 9⅜ × 12¼. 23580-7 Pa. $6.95

THE JOURNAL OF HENRY D. THOREAU, edited by Bradford Torrey, F. H. Allen. Complete reprinting of 14 volumes, 1837–61, over two million words; the sourcebooks for *Walden*, etc. Definitive. All original sketches, plus 75 photographs. 1,804pp. 8½ × 12¼. 20312-3, 20313-1 Cloth., Two-vol. set $120.00

CASTLES: THEIR CONSTRUCTION AND HISTORY, Sidney Toy. Traces castle development from ancient roots. Nearly 200 photographs and drawings illustrate moats, keeps, baileys, many other features. Caernarvon, Dover Castles, Hadrian's Wall, Tower of London, dozens more. 256pp. 5⅜ × 8¼.
24898-4 Pa. $6.95

CATALOG OF DOVER BOOKS

AMERICAN CLIPPER SHIPS: 1833–1858, Octavius T. Howe & Frederick C. Matthews. Fully-illustrated, encyclopedic review of 352 clipper ships from the period of America's greatest maritime supremacy. Introduction. 109 halftones. 5 black-and-white line illustrations. Index. Total of 928pp. 5⅜ × 8½.
25115-2, 25116-0 Pa., Two-vol. set $17.90

TOWARDS A NEW ARCHITECTURE, Le Corbusier. Pioneering manifesto by great architect, near legendary founder of "International School." Technical and aesthetic theories, views on industry, economics, relation of form to function, "mass-production spirit," much more. Profusely illustrated. Unabridged translation of 13th French edition. Introduction by Frederick Etchells. 320pp. 6⅛ × 9¼. (Available in U.S. only)
25023-7 Pa. $8.95

THE BOOK OF KELLS, edited by Blanche Cirker. Inexpensive collection of 32 full-color, full-page plates from the greatest illuminated manuscript of the Middle Ages, painstakingly reproduced from rare facsimile edition. Publisher's Note. Captions. 32pp. 9⅜ × 12¼.
24345-1 Pa. $4.95

BEST SCIENCE FICTION STORIES OF H. G. WELLS, H. G. Wells. Full novel *The Invisible Man*, plus 17 short stories: "The Crystal Egg," "Aepyornis Island," "The Strange Orchid," etc. 303pp. 5⅜ × 8½. (Available in U.S. only)
21531-8 Pa. $6.95

AMERICAN SAILING SHIPS: Their Plans and History, Charles G. Davis. Photos, construction details of schooners, frigates, clippers, other sailcraft of 18th to early 20th centuries—plus entertaining discourse on design, rigging, nautical lore, much more. 137 black-and-white illustrations. 240pp. 6⅛ × 9¼.
24658-2 Pa. $6.95

ENTERTAINING MATHEMATICAL PUZZLES, Martin Gardner. Selection of author's favorite conundrums involving arithmetic, money, speed, etc., with lively commentary. Complete solutions. 112pp. 5⅜ × 8½.
25211-6 Pa. $2.95

THE WILL TO BELIEVE, HUMAN IMMORTALITY, William James. Two books bound together. Effect of irrational on logical, and arguments for human immortality. 402pp. 5⅜ × 8½.
20291-7 Pa. $7.95

THE HAUNTED MONASTERY and THE CHINESE MAZE MURDERS, Robert Van Gulik. 2 full novels by Van Gulik continue adventures of Judge Dee and his companions. An evil Taoist monastery, seemingly supernatural events; overgrown topiary maze that hides strange crimes. Set in 7th-century China. 27 illustrations. 328pp. 5⅜ × 8½.
23502-5 Pa. $6.95

CELEBRATED CASES OF JUDGE DEE (DEE GOONG AN), translated by Robert Van Gulik. Authentic 18th-century Chinese detective novel; Dee and associates solve three interlocked cases. Led to Van Gulik's own stories with same characters. Extensive introduction. 9 illustrations. 237pp. 5⅜ × 8½.
23337-5 Pa. $4.95

Prices subject to change without notice.
Available at your book dealer or write for free catalog to Dept. GI, Dover Publications, Inc., 31 East 2nd St., Mineola, N.Y. 11501. Dover publishes more than 175 books each year on science, elementary and advanced mathematics, biology, music, art, literary history, social sciences and other areas.